Chinese Acrobatics
Through the Ages

Chinese Acrobatics Through the Ages

FU QIFENG

FOREIGN LANGUAGES PRESS   BEIJING

First edition   1985

Translated by
Ouyang Caiwei and Rhoda Stockwell

ISBN 0-8351-1037-8

Published by Foreign Languages Press
24 Baiwanzhuang Road, Beijing, China
Printed by Foreign Languages Printing House
19 West Chegongzhuang Road, Beijing, China

Distributed by China International Book Trading Corporation
(Guoji Shudian), P.O. Box 399, Beijing, China

Printed in the People's Republic of China

Contents

Preface

World-famous for its distinctive national style and superb skills, Chinese acrobatics is one of the world's earliest performing arts making use of gymnastic skills. We may trace its history back to primitive society. Counting from the time when it gradually became a fairly integrated performing art, it has a history of more than 2,000 years. During this long period it has gone through many vicissitudes and has been persecuted by the feudal ruling class on many occasions. But, taking root in the fertile soil of the people, it has consistently retained its vitality handed down from generation to generation.

Several thousand years ago, the forefathers of the Chinese nation, inhabitants of the Yellow River valley, created the acrobatic arts, drawing examples from labour, fighting, religious sacrifice and other aspects of daily life. In feudal society Chinese acrobatics traversed a course from the commoners to the court and back to the commoners. With the change of dynasties and the development and merging of China's various nationalities, its forms of performance have steadily become richer and more varied. Over the past century it has assimilated favourable factors from foreign acrobatics and has created many new items. During the 33 years since liberation, Chinese acrobatics has rediscovered and improved on traditional numbers and weeded through the old to bring forth the new. Hence it has assumed an entirely new look on stage and has won the praise of audiences at home and abroad.

The history of Chinese acrobatics is a component of the history of Chinese culture and art. Voluminous Chinese books, paintings preserved in different dynasties, stone and brick carvings, funerary objects in tombs, murals and terracotta figures, provide valuable data for our understanding of ancient Chinese acrobatics. We may see from such data that most items of contemporary Chinese acrobatics, at home and abroad, although with an entirely new appearance after countless changes, can trace their "roots" back to ancient acrobatics.

Based on the best of existing data in written language and from ancient artifacts, this book probes into the development of ancient Chinese acrobatics. It attempts to give a concise, general survey of contemporary Chinese acrobatics. Thus, the readers may obtain a general idea of how Chinese acrobatics, with its long history, has developed from a burgeoning art to its present condition.

1. The Origin of Acrobatics

(*Prehistory to 206 B.C.*)

As early as the New Stone Age the Chinese people created a primitive performing art in the course of hunting, gathering, stock-breeding, fighting and offering sacrifices to gods and ancestors. At first it was just the simple imitation of various activities, but later was refined and beautified. Usually, this primitive performing art was a show combining singing, dancing and other entertainments. The "Ancient Music Section" of *Lü Shi Chun Qiu* (*Lü's Spring and Autumn Annals*), written in the Warring States Period (475-221 B.C.), records: "The music of the Getian tribe in ancient times was performed in the following fashion — Three men, holding ox tails in their hands, sang eight melodies and danced to their rhythm: 1. Wishing mankind happiness. 2. Black birds (expressing totem worship). 3. Wishing luxuriant growth of plants and trees. 4. Wishing rich harvests of the five grain crops. 5. Paying respects to the heaven for providing ample food and clothing. 6. Extolling the exploits of the God of Heaven. 7. Thanking the favours of the earth. 8. Wishing the propagation of birds and animals.

Getian was the name of a remote tribe in Chinese legends. This form of singing and dancing while holding ox tails included animal masquerades in acrobatics, while the content of "singing eight melodies" portrayed daily work such as hunting, stock-

breeding and farming as well as offering sacrifices to heaven, the earth and ancestors.

As society developed, the primitive performing arts gradually branched out into instrumental music, song and dance. The performance stressing gymnastic skills was the beginning of acrobatics. In ancient times acrobatics were closely linked with all human activities. Work, fighting between tribes, religious sacrifices and other daily activities all had their corresponding acrobatic movements. The evolution and development of these movements have made Chinese acrobatic art varied and fascinating.

Acrobatics did not become an independent performing art until the Spring and Autumn (770-476 B.C.) and Warring States periods. During this time the invention and use of iron utensils brought about great advances in technology so that agriculture, handicraft and stockbreeding made rapid progress. Then tremendous changes took place in Chinese society. From primitive society it entered into slave society and then made the transition into feudal society. "A hundred schools of thought" contended in the realm of culture and ideology. The development of the performing arts manifested itself in the finer division of labour day by day. With regard to performers alone, a number of them specialized in singing and dancing, while others were jesters and musicians. Although there is no historical record regarding what acrobatic performers were called, quite a number of descriptions of acrobatic performances can be found in books. It was also during this period that acrobatic arts went from the common people into the homes of dukes and marquesses and then into the court of the Qin Dynasty (221-207 B.C.)

The Origin of "Juggling Boards"

"Juggling Boards", or the art of juggling with the hands, often presented on the modern Chinese acrobatic stage, is the earliest acrobatic number known to date. It can be traced back to the New Stone Age. At that time hunters, from primitive tribes, frequently used a piece of hunting gear which is called a "boomerang" by archeologists. When a hunter discovered a bird, an animal or other game, he threw a "boomerang". Twirling, it flew towards the target. If it failed to hit the object, it came back to the hunter's hands so that he might throw it a second time. Such a "boomerang" is reportedly still in use among some tribes in Africa, Australia and India. The Mongolians in north China call it "Bulu".

Although using the "boomerang" for hunting required superb skill, it was not an acrobatic performance. In earliest times, it was often necessary for people to pass on knowledge and exchange skills, so that those who were more expert frequently demonstrated their skills to others. Such demonstration performances gradually appeared at the gatherings of primitive tribes. If many experts gave such demonstrations, there would be contests among them. This turned a performance into a contest, both improving skills and imbuing the performance with a rich recreational flavour. Contests often turned production skills into acrobatic arts. The annual "Nadam" fair in Inner Mongolia, north China, has retained the tradition of earliest times. There are horse racing, wrestling, contests of strength and, sometimes, "Bulu" contests at the Nadam fair.

Later, the "boomerang" was no longer used for hunting but rather as a piece of stage property for acrobatic performances. Artists used it to perform a variety of juggling feats for people's entertainment. On stage an acrobat juggled as many as three, five or even eight boomerangs, throwing them in order and catching them one by one. He might make the "boomerang" fall on any part of his body, the innovated "boomerang" twirling a long while after falling. The "boomerang" became known as a "juggling board". The "juggling board" has a history of 1,000 years in China. *Dong Jing Meng Hua Lu* (*Memories of the Eastern Capital*) written by Meng Yuanlao during the Southern Song Dynasty (A.D. 1127-1279) recorded performances with this item. The author recollected the appearance of the capital Bianjing (present-day Kaifeng in Henan Province), as well as its customs and habits and the cultural life of its inhabitants during the Northern Song Dynasty (A.D. 960-1127).

Similar to "Juggling Boards", other acrobatic feats developed from the skills of using tools or weapons including "Target Shooting with Bow", "Flying Tridents", "Exercises with a Heavy Halberd", "Bending Stiff Bows", and "Swinging Meteors". There are also other acrobatic activities which have been developed without resorting to the implements or skills of labour. Among these are "Rope Walking" drawn

— 2 —

from climbing up high mountains or precipitous cliffs and "Pole Balancing" drawn from tree and pole climbing (Figure 1).

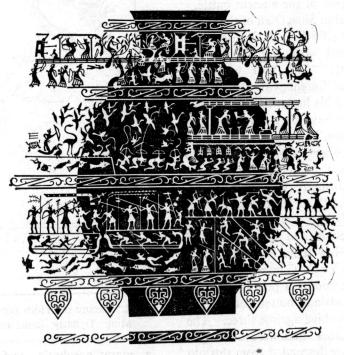

1. Copy of the decoration on a Warring States ewer depicting feasting, merry-making, fishing, hunting and battle. Unearthed in Chengdu, Sichuan

"Chi You's Games" and "Horn Butting Games"

Chinese acrobatic performances before the Qin (221-207 B.C.) and Han (206 B.C.-A.D. 220) dynasties were called "Horn Butting Games". They originated from tribal wars on Chinese territory in ancient times. So, fighting among our ancestors was also one of the sources of the acrobatic arts.

It is said that around 2,550 B.C., a fierce war was fought between the Yellow Emperor, a great figure in ancient Chinese legends and forefather of the Chinese nation, and Chi You, leader of the Lis in the south. At the beginning of the war, Chi You and his 81 brothers with heads of bronze and foreheads

of iron launched a terrifying offensive. They had horns on their heads, ate sand and stone, and mounted on clouds to cross mountains. They conjured up wind and thick fog which blurred the vision of the Yellow Emperor's soldiers, and he suffered several defeats. The Yellow Emperor invented a vehicle with a wooden figure always pointing to the south, no matter which way the vehicle turned. He then persuaded fierce animals on earth and huge dragons in heaven to fight on his side. After uniting several tribes and experiencing many hardships, he defeated Chi You and his 81 brothers.

Later, the Yellow Emperor's descendants

cherished the memory of the glorious exploits of their forefathers and created "Chi You's Games" in imitation of the ancient battle.

The great historian Sima Qian of the Western Han Dynasty (206 B.C.-A.D. 24) wrote in his monumental work *Shi Ji* (*Records of the Historian*): "Chi You who had horns on his head fought with the Yellow Emperor and used his horns to butt people. Chi You's Games have been recreated and performed in Jizhou."

The *Shu Yi Ji* (*Bizarre Tales*) attributed to Ren Fang, a man of letters during the Southern and Northern Dynasties, (A.D. 420-589), describes "Chi You's Games" in Jizhou more explicitly: Chi You "used his horns to butt people and they could not withstand this. Now there is an entertainment called 'Chi You's Games' in Jizhou. In the games, the common people wore ox horns on their heads and butted each other, two against two or three against three. The 'Horn Butting Games' that were developed in the Han Dynasty descended from this old tradition." As we see from these records, "Chi You's Games" were a very popular contest of strength among the people (Figure 2).

As a matter of fact, the "Horn Butting Games" in the Qin and Han dynasties represented diverse entertainments stressing feats of physical prowess. Feats such as weightlifting, bearing loads, wrestling and martial arts are important components of acrobatics. Modern acrobatic performances contain many feats of physical prowess such as "Pole Balancing", "Bending Stiff Bows" and "Exercises with a Heavy Halberd" as well as "A Human Pagoda of Seven Acrobats". Performers who act as the base of a pyramid

2. Picture of "Horn Butting Games" in a Ming Dynasty collection of woodcuts.

in many acrobatic performances require much physical ability.

"Horn Butting Games" tracing back to the legend of the Yellow Emperor battling Chi You was the earliest hallmark which distinguished acrobatic art from other branches of art. Although we cannot rely on ancient legends as accurate data, it is our belief that feats of physical prowess as evidenced in acrobatics gradually came into being in the course of ancient wars. They portray images of bravery and reflect men's confidence in conquering nature and defeating the enemy. These forms of acrobatics still appear on the acrobatic stage and are loved by the people.

Animal Shows and Animal Masquerade Shows

As primitive people improved their ability to conquer nature, they gradually turned from fishing, hunting and gathering wild fruits and plants to stockbreeding and farming. Records of domesticating animals often appeared in ancient books. At first, people domesticated animals to meet their needs for food, clothing and sacrificial ceremonies. For instance, Lei Zu, the Yellow Emperor's wife, raised silkworms to provide people with silk for clothing. Later, people raised animals to work for man and fight in wars.

Once people had sufficient food and clothing, they required entertainment, so the domesticated animals were driven to festivals or tribal celebrations. *Shang Shu* (*The Book of History*), a collection of Chinese historical documents in early times reportedly compiled by Confucius, records: "As I struck and played a stone instrument, a hundred animals danced to the musical rhythm." It described that in the 21st century B.C., an official in charge of music named Kui who worked under Yao could play musical instruments made of stone to accompany the dancing of different kinds of animals (Figure 3). Yao was the leader of the tribal league in the later period of the patriarchal clan society and was

honoured as one of the three sage emperors in early times.

Just like the exploits of semi-god and semi-human heroes in the Greek poet Homer's epics, the above-mentioned records also contain many mythological legends. Historical books record that in fighting against Chi You, Yellow Emperor drove bears, tigers, leopards and other fierce animals to charge and smash enemy positions. Some people believed that the Yellow Emperor mobilized those tribes with fierce animals as totems to join him in battle.

Although it was written, "A hundred animals danced to the musical rhythm" at the time of Emperor Yao, it was, in fact, people dancing, disguised as animals.

In the 18th century B.C., in the late Xia Dynasty, there were already performances of "making horses dance" at court. Such taming of horses to make them dance was, without doubt, the earliest and most simple circus show.

Owing to their strong desire to tame birds and animals and conquer nature, people dressed in animal pelts and bird feathers and used their hands and feet to imitate the movements of birds and animals. What was previously described as "people of a tribe

3. Copy of the picture of animal taming on a ewer of the Warring States Period with hunting designs.

named Getian danced, holding ox tails in their hands" and "a hundred animals danced to the musical rhythm", all belonged to this category. *Shi Jing* (*The Book of Odes*), a collection of ancient Chinese songs, describes a presentation by a young woman masquerading as a bird:

> Through winter's cold, and summer weather,
> This maiden, so lively and gay,
> Must rush to the arena, and pass the day
> In brandishing her egret feather.
> And while her footsteps beat the ground
> In cadence, as her fan she swings,
> With music all the precinct rings,
> And drums and tambourines resound.

As one of the folk songs during the Eastern Zhou Dynasty (770-221 B.C.) collected in *The Book of Odes*, it illustrates that dancing in the disguise of birds and animals was a frequent occurrence among the people.

Ancient entertainment performed in the form of animal masquerades was prevalent at sacrificial rites. These rites reflected that ancient people did not understand natural phenomena and attempted to conquer nature with the aid of supernatural power. On the other hand, these rites were for amusement as well as in commemoration of the exploits of their ancestors. For example, "Dances of Exorcism" was typical of such shows. At the end of every year all people tried to chase off plague-causing devils, wished for prosperity good health in the following year. The procession for chasing off devils and pests was led by a man named Fang Xiang, an official in charge of this work. With four eyes on his golden face, he was dressed in a red robe, and held a dagger-axe and a shield in his hands. Behind him were men masquerading as a dozen kinds of fierce animals. In the rear were more than 100 children wearing red caps and playing tambourine-like small drums. The mighty procession shouted, to chase off devils and pests, and the atmosphere was grand and solemn. The people believed the plague-causing devils would be panic-stricken and flee when they met this procession. From activities such as "Dances of Exorcism" were evolved many acrobatic performances, including the "Lion Dance" and the "Flying Tridents".

Witches or sorcerers sponsored sacrificial rites similar to "Dances of Exorcism" to make people believe in their supernatural powers. *Chu Ci* (*Elegies of Chu*), a collection of poems of the kingdom of Chu, with the works of China's earliest great poet Qu Yuan (c. 340-278 B.C.) as its main body, tells of the miraculous skills or magical power of witches and sorcerers who promoted the development of primitive magic.

"Rang Hitting" — Origin of Shooting Items

"Rang Hitting" was a game often played in the fields. It is said that at the time of Yao, peace prevailed across the country and people were happy and prosperous. An old man, hitting "rang", sang the following song which has been recorded in ancient books:

> With the sunrise, I begin to work,
> With the sunset, I take a rest,

> I dig a well for drinking water,
> I till the fields for food.
> What can the king do to me?

According to the records in the *Tai Ping Yu Lan* (*Taiping Imperial Encyclopaedia*), an imperial collection of reference books classified according to different subjects compiled between A.D. 977 and 981 during the North-

4. Picture of "Rang Hitting" in a Ming Dynasty collection of woodcuts.

the time of Yao. Archaeologically it belongs to the time of the Longshan Culture in the late Neolithic Age, later than that of the "boomerang". It was done in the fields but had no direct relationship to farm production. It appears to be a game that was played during breaks in the work day. The skill of "Rang Hitting" depended upon accuracy in throwing. The shape of the "rang", wide in the front and narrow at the back, reminds one of the stones thrown by primitive people, but it was made of wood, resembling the wedge of later times. The employment of commonly used utensils as throwing objects, developed from "Rang Hitting", is what makes Chinese acrobatics brim with the rich flavour of everyday life.

Accuracy in throwing objects required in the game of "Rang Hitting" is an important factor in acrobatic skills. We can see traces of this game in "Throwing Arrows into a Wine Pot" of the Han Dynasty (260 B.C.- A.D. 220), the children's game of "Throwing Tiles and Stones" and "Throwing Bricks" of the Song Dynasty (960-1279). "Striking at Tiles" (a pile of tiles heaped high on a performer's head and another performer smashes the tiles without hurting the head), and "Juggling Five Stone Locks" of the Ming Dynasty (1368-1644), as well as the "Knife Throwing" and "Whip Feats" of modern times trace back to "Rang Hitting", also.

ern Song Dynasty, "rang" was made of a strip of wood in the shape of the sole of a shoe; it was wide in the front and narrow at the back, about 50 cm. long and 10 cm. wide. Prior to the game, a "rang" was planted in the ground and another "rang" was thrown from a spot 30 or 40 steps away. Hitting the "rang" planted on the ground was considered superb skill (Figure 4).

The game of "Rang Hitting" appeared at

From Commoners to Rich, Powerful Families

Acrobatics was at first a folk art. It originated from people's daily life, including their work, battles and sacrificial rites. During the Warring States Period, acrobatics became widespread. It was believed that practising acrobatics could steel people's will and increase their physical strength and the accuracy of their movements.

"The Secret of Life", Chapter 19 in *Zhuang Zi* (*The Book of Zhuang Zi*), one of the Taoist classics, records the story of a hunchback catching cicadas and illustrates this belief.

When Confucius passed through the state of Chu, he came to a forest where he he saw a hunchback catching cicadas with a long stick as though with his hand.

"How dexterous you are!" cried Confucius. "Have you any way of doing this?"

"I have a way", replied the hunchback. "This comes as a result of long practice. I practised balancing two balls one on top of the other on the tip of the stick for five or six months. If they do not fall, I do not miss many cicadas. When I can balance three balls, it is as though I caught the cicadas with my hand."

It requires superb skill to balance three balls, and the balancing of balls, one on top of the other, as done by the hunchback, resembles "Balancing Eggs on a Chopstick" in modern acrobatics. It can be conceived that there were not a few folk artists similar to the hunchback during the Warring States Period who promoted the progress of acrobatic art.

It is noteworthy that during the Spring and Autumn and the Warring States periods there were actually acrobats who demonstrated their skills on a battlefield where two troops fought each other.

"Xu Wugui", Chapter 24 in *Zhuang Zi*, recounts: "Yi Liao of Shinan juggled balls, and the conflict between two houses was eliminated."

Xiong Yiliao of the Chu State was good at "Juggling Balls". Once, in a battle between the states of Chu and Song, the troops of the two sides were confronting each other in a fight at close quarters. Yiliao appeared in front of the Chu troops and calmly, in the face of the enemy's axes and spears, juggled nine balls at the same time. His superb performance stupefied the officers and warriors. The Song troops fled helter-skelter without fighting and the Chu troops won a complete victory. This is a unique example of the use of an artist's miraculous skill to defeat the opponent by a surprise move. But this story shows the great popularity of acrobatic art and how people were completely convinced by artists with marvellous skills. Because folk art was made use of by rulers, acrobatics

5. "Lan Zi Juggling Swords" in a Ming Dynasty collection of woodcuts.

gradually advanced from the commoners into the mansions of nobles and high officials.

Lie Zi (*The Book of Lie Zi*), a philosophical work attributed to Lie Yukou of the Warring States Period, records that in the Spring and Autumn Period, Lan Zi, of the state of Song, presented a performance for the ruler. He could run to and fro on very high stilts and could also juggle seven swords (Figure 5). Duke Yuan, of the state of Song, appreciated Lan Zi's great skill and gave him generous rewards.

Guo Yu (*Discourse on the States*) was reportedly written by Zuoqiu Ming to record mainly the sayings of nobles in different states during the last years of the Western Zhou Dynasty (c. 11th century B.C.-770 B.C.) and in the Spring and Autumn Period. It reports an acrobatic performance of a midget climbing a pole. This refers to a buffoon dwarf at the court of the state of Jin who demonstrated the skill of climbing up a pole before many spectators (Figure 6).

These are the earliest records of performances of court acrobats found so far.

6. Rubbing of a stone relief in a Han Dynasty tomb in Feicheng, Shandong Province, depicting "Juggling Balls" and "Pole Climbing", and copy of a detail.

Earliest Vocal Mimicry

In the Warring States Period there remained only seven powerful states — Qi, Chu, Yan, Han, Zhao, Wei and Qin — in rivalry with one another for conquest and annexation. To attain this purpose, the feudal rulers of the various states had to recruit talented people. This led to the emergence of "scholars" — a stratum of the rising landlord class. As these scholars travelled from ruler to ruler and lived under the patronage of the lords, they were known as "guests" or "proteges". Each had his own strong points and was loyal to his patron. It was prevalent among the rulers and nobles to "patronize scholars" on a widespread scale. For instance, Lord Mengchang, a noble of the Qi State, patronized more than 1,000 "guests". The story of "cock-crow and passing off as a dog", China's earliest story about vocal mimicry, describes the skill of the proteges under Lord Mengchang's patronage.

Around 300 B.C., King Zhao of the Qin State was afraid that the state of Qi would become too powerful, so he tricked Lord Mengchang of Qi and his entire household into coming to the Qin State. He then put them under house arrest with a plan to kill them. Lord Mengchang consulted with the proteges in his company to figure out a plan to extricate themselves from the danger. They decided to ask the favourite concubine of King Zhao of Qin to say something in Lord Mengchang's favour. He found a protege who could pass off as a dog to go stealthily into the Qin palace room deep in the night and bring out the rare "white-fox fur coat", which he had offered the king of Qin as a gift, and give it to the concubine instead. As a result she interceded on Lord Mengchang's behalf and King Zhao released him. Lord Mengchang, knowing that the Qin king was capricious, galloped off, leaving the Qin State that very night. The Qin king regretted his decision and sent soldiers to chase after Lord Mengchang, who reached the Hangu Pass, a strategic fortification at the Qin frontier, by midnight. But the pass was closed and there was a rule that no one might go through before cock-crow. The situation was critical with the pass in front of them and the pursuing soldiers behind. At that moment one of his proteges imitated the crow of a cock which set all the other cocks to crowing. The soldiers guarding the pass thought that it was already daybreak and opened the gates to let the fugitives through. Thus Lord Mengchang and company succeeded in returning to their own state.

This story of "cock-crow and passing off as a dog" was recorded in the famous *Records of the Historian*. The proteges skilled at these tricks were probably acrobats of that time. Their vocal mimicry had attained the level of sounding genuine, otherwise the other cocks would not have crowed. It can thus be seen that vocal mimicry was burgeoning more than 2,000 years ago.

King Wu of Qin "Lifted the Tripod and Broke His Kneecap"

In the Spring and Autumn and Warring States periods, there were continual wars between the states in the attempt to annex each others' territories. A trend to encourage physical prowess prevailed which led to the appearance of many "scholars" who were strongmen. For instance, Xia Yu of the Wei State could lift 1,000 *jun* (one *jun* equals to present-day 15 kilogrammes) and pull off the tail of a live ox (Figure 7). Confucius' father Shuliang He had unrivalled strength. He could lift up the 500-kilogramme heavy city gates to let his men storm into the city. A man named Di Humi could storm enemy positions, wielding a huge cart wheel. His military feats provided material for acrobatics. There have been similar acrobatic items called "Wheel Wielding" since the Han Dynasty (Figure 8).

In the Warring States Period, the state of Qin became powerful and prosperous as a result of the reforms initiated by Shang Yang, its prime minister, who promoted agriculture and encouraged soldiers to distinguish themselves on the battlefield. Consequently, many heroes of various states went there and strongmen, such as Ren Bi and Wu Huo who were tripod-lifting experts, thronged to Xian-

1. Music, dancing and acrobatics figurines from the Western Han
Dynasty, unearthed from a Han tomb in Jinan, Shandong Province.

2. *The Queen of Song Touring with Her Entourage*, a Tang Dynasty mural in the Mogao Grottoes in Dunhuang.

3. Tang Dynasty silver ewer modelled after a leather bag and decorated with the design of a dancing horse with a wine cup in its mouth, unearthed from the southern outskirts of Xi'an, Shaanxi Province.

4. Tang Dynasty earthen figurines performing the "Lion Dance", unearthed from a Tang tomb in Turpan, Xinjiang.

5. Tang Dynasty mural in an ancient palace in Tibet depicting the "Lion Dance".

6. "Pole Balancing" in a Song Dynasty mural (copy) in Dunhuang.

7. Detail of *Picture of Lantern Festival at
the New Year*, a Ming Dynasty painting.

8. Wrestling as depicted in the Qing Dynasty painting
Four Sports Events at a Banquet at the Frontier (detail).

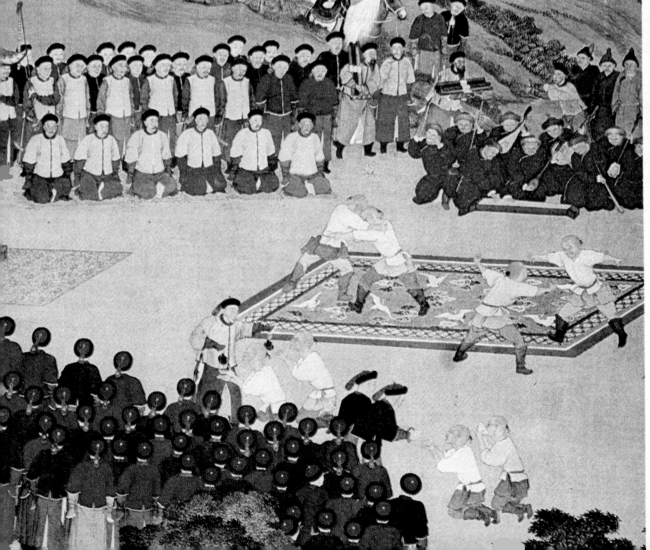

9. A Qing Dynasty picture of folk horsemanship.

10. "Rope Walking" in the Ming Dynasty painting *The Riverside Scene at the Qingming Festival* (detail).

11. "Flying Trident" in the Ming Dynasty painting *The Riverside Scene at the Qingming Festival* (detail).

12. "Juggling Properties with the Feet" in the Ming Dynasty painting *The Riverside Scene at the Qingming Festival* (detail).

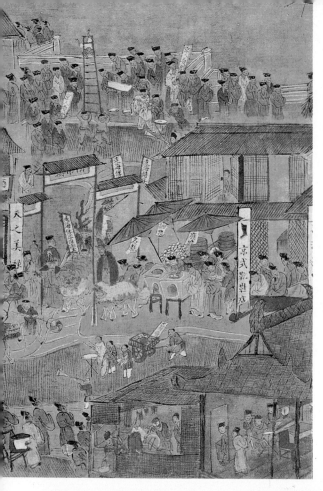

13. Performance of the "Lion Dance" and "Scaling Ladders" in a strolling acrobatic procession in the Ming Dynasty painting *Lively Procession in the Southern Capital* (detail).

14. Performance of stunts on stilts and miscellaneous feats in a strolling acrobatic procession in the Ming Dynasty painting *Lively Procession in the Southern Capital* (detail).

15. "Conjuring" in a Qing
Dynasty genre painting.

16. "Plate Spinning" in a
Qing Dynasty genre painting.

17. "Tamed Bear" in a Qing Dynasty genre painting.

18. "Tamed Monkey and Sheep" in a Qing Dynasty genre painting.

19. "Jar Tricks" in a Qing Dynasty genre painting.

7. Rubbing of a stone carving in a Han Dynasty tomb in Xuzhou Prefecture, Jiangsu Province, showing men subduing a tiger, up-rooting a tree, shouldering an ox and lifting a stone mortar.

8. Copy of a mural in a Han Dynasty tomb in Liaoyang showing wheel juggling and plate spinning.

yang, capital of the Qin State. Even King Wu of the Qin State often took part in lifting tripods and physical combats.

In 307 B.C. the ambitious King Wu of Qin went with courtiers to Luoyang, the capital of the Eastern Zhou Dynasty (770-221 B.C.) to see the nine tripods which were said to be divine vessels handed down from early times when King Yu succeeded in guiding the flood-waters into the rivers and out to the sea. They symbolized the rule of the Son of Heaven — the emperor. Seeing and inquir-ing about the nine tripods really meant eye-ing the throne of the emperor of Zhuo and attempting to supersede him. At the time of seeing the nine tripods, King Wu of Qin com-peted with Meng Yue, a famous strongman of that time, by lifting up a tripod to display his supernatural strength. The heavy iron tripod exerted such great pressure that the King's eyes bled, and he died instantly when the tripod fell and broke his kneecap. The strongman Meng Yue who had competed with King Wu of Qin in the event was executed. This incident has been historically recorded as "lifting up the tripod and breaking his kneecap".

People in subsequent dynasties have shown great esteem and admiration for the miracu-lous strength of these tripod-lifting heroes. "Tripod Lifting" was often cited in the Han Dynasty's "Hundred Entertainments". An-cient performers of feats of physical prowess honoured and paid homage to Wu Huo and Xia Yu as founders of "Tripod Lifting".

"Tripod Lifting" only vanished after the Tang (618-907) and Song (960-1279) dynasties. Replacing it were new contests of strength such as "Bending Stiff Bows", "Kick-ing a Stone Load", "Juggling Stone Locks" and "Juggling Jars". These new items came into being because the tripod gradually lost its function and bows, stone loads, stone locks and jars and other such stage properties were more directly linked with the daily life of the people. Also, the sport of weight-lifting and juggling jars and stone locks were more suitable for displaying strength and acrobatic skill and attracted larger audiences.

Court Acrobatics in the Qin Dynasty

In 221 B.C., Qin Shi Huang (First Emperor of the Qin Dynasty), a statesman of great talent and bold vision, annexed six other states and unified China. He founded the Qin Dynasty — the first centralized, autocratic feudal dynasty in Chinese history.

Unified state power brought the cultures of the six states to Xianyang, the capital of the Qin Dynasty (221-207 B.C.). Acrobatic numbers were concentrated into full-length variety shows known as "Jiao Di", or literally, "Horn Butting".

Both the First Emperor and his son the Second Emperor of Qin indulged themselves in pleasures and brought together court performers, numbering several thousand, including singers, dancers, musicians, actors, and quite a number of acrobats.

There are few historical records about acrobatic performances at the Qin court, but Qin acrobatics were noteworthy, both in quantity and as fascinating performances. A passage in the "Biography of Li Si" in *Records of the Historian* gives an example of a spectacular acrobatic performance at the Qin court.

In 209 B.C. the Second Emperor of Qin watched a spectacle of "Horn Butting" at the Sweet Spring Palace. Prime Minister Li Si, although he had been of great help to the founding of the Qin Dynasty, was to be executed. Li Si asked to see the emperor who was watching a performance and so ignored his request. The performance probably contained numbers such as "Juggling with the Hands", "Magic", "Vocal Mimicry", "Animal Shows" and "Animal Masquerade". Because of the abundance of acrobatic items, a grand acrobatic performance was presented.

Qin was a short dynasty, lasting only 15 years from its founding to downfall. But, viewing it from the history of acrobatics, it laid a favourable foundation for the flowering of the "Hundred Entertainments" in the Han Dynasty.

2. The "Hundred Entertainments" of the Han Dynasty

(206 B.C.-A.D. 220)

The autocratic Qin Dynasty collapsed after the reign of only two emperors. Replacing it was the Western Han Dynasty (206 B.C.-A.D. 24), a dynasty that pursued the policy of "letting the nation recuperate, grow and engage in production," and the nation gradually became prosperous and powerful. During the rule of Emperor Wu named Liu Che (140-87 B.C.) economy thrived, the country became a mighty power, people lived in peace and stability, and civilization flourished. The emperor used diplomacy and military force to expand his territory. He sent Zhang Qian as an envoy to the Western Regions (a general reference in the Han Dynasty to areas beyond present-day Yumen pass in Gansu Province) to promote cultural exchange and enhance the friendship between the people of China and the people in Central Asia. With this exchange, Chinese acrobatic art also made great progress and flowered.

The performing arts of the Han Dynasty were divided into court entertainments and common entertainments. Court entertainments, also called ritual entertainment, consisted of government-sponsored music and dance. Common or popular entertainments were composed of folk music and dance. Court entertainments, presented at ceremonies in palaces and halls, were monotonous and stereotyped. Common entertainments, coming from the people, were lively and vivacious. As common entertainments had a rich and varied contents, they were also called the "Hundred Entertainments". They were composed of activities for amusement such as acrobatics, singing and dancing, martial arts, music and opera. Historical records show that acrobatics accounted for a great majority of the performances which enjoyed great popularity among the people and were later summoned by the supreme rulers of the Han Dynasty. When presented at the imperial court, these performances were known as "Fish and Dragons and Competitive Games".

The Han Dynasty actually consisted of two dynasties in Chinese history. The Western Han Dynasty was founded by Liu Bang, known as Emperor Gao Zu, in 206 B.C. with its capital in Chang'an (present-day Xi'an in Shaanxi Province). The Eastern Han Dynasty was established by Liu Xiu known as Emperor Guang Wu with its capital in Luoyang (in present-day Henan Province). As acrobatics flowered in both the Western and Eastern Han dynasties, they were called the "Hundred Entertainments" of the Han Dynasty.

There is a wealth of data about the Han "Hundred Entertainments". Written data include descriptions in *Records of the Historian* and *Han Shu* (*History of the Han Dynasty*), as well as in *Xi Jing Fu* (*Rhyme-Prose on the Western Capital*) by Zhang Heng of the Eastern Han Dynasty, which depicted the luxurious life of the ruling class of the Western Han Dynasty. Other data are obtained from a great number of stone sculptures, brick carvings, pottery figures, murals and other unearthed ancient materials. The areas where these antiques were dug up show that acrobatics in the Han Dynasty were popular from the coast of the Bohai Sea in the east to the plains of Shaanxi Province in the west, from outside the Great Wall in the north to the Yangtze valley in the south.

Folk Acrobatics Depicted on Relics from
Western Han Tombs

People in the Han Dynasty were very fond of recreation so there were often performances of the "Hundred Entertainments" at festivals and celebrations. At banquets and gatherings the families of nobles and wealthy people also frequently used performances presented by musicians, dancers and actors to entertain guests. Two-thousand-year-old pottery figurines of musicians, dancers and acrobats (Colour plate 1) unearthed on Jinan's outskirts in Shandong Province depict in a concise and vivid manner the folk acrobatic performances of the Western Han Dynasty.

Fourteen acrobats are shown in a performance of the most essential acrobatic skills such as handstands and backward waist-bending in calisthenics. The performers appear graceful and poised in their movements to the musical accompaniment of Jian drums (a small drum on a stand with three feet, which traces back to the Zhou Dynasty), small durms, bells, *se* (zither-like, 25-stringed plucked instrument) and *sheng* (a reed pipe wind instrument). This illustrates the rhythmic beauty and high artistry of the Western Han Dynasty acrobatics.

The "Picture of Feasting and Hundred Entertainments" on Han Dynasty brick reliefs excavated at Yangzishan in Chengdu, Sichuan Province (Figures 9 & 10), "Feasting in Celebration of Rich Harvest", a mural at Bangzitai in Liaoning Province and "Picture of the Hundred Entertainments", a mural in a tomb of Horinger in Inner Mongolia, are representative of the illustrations of acrobatic performances at banquets during the Western Han Dynasty. At that time acrobatic performances were presented at feasts in celebration of excellent harvests or happy occasions. The host sat at a prominent seat in a hall and was surrounded by guests. The centre of the hall was reserved for the acrobatic performance. As seen in the above-mentioned brick reliefs and murals, the items included feats of physical prowess such as wielding cart wheels, traditional juggling of balls and other feats of juggling, new numbers such as plate spinning, acts with trained animals, dances on seven trays and waving flags on tall poles.

It is noteworthy that the performances

9. Rubbing of a brick relief from the Han Dynasty depicting feasting and the "Hundred Entertainments". Unearthed in Chengdu, Sichuan Province.

10. Picture of feasting and the "Hundred Entertainments" on a stone carving found in a Han Dynasty tomb in Chengdu, Sichuan Province (copy).

put on at feasts among the commoners were the same as those presented in the court performances of the Western Han Dynasty, with only slight differences. This illustrates that acrobatic art originated from the people, developed among the people, and had great vitality, resulting in its popularity among the ruling class. But, differing from other forms of literature and art, acrobatics did not become rigid after entering the court, and therefore, did not decline with the downfall of any feudal dynasty.

Grand Performances at Emperor Wu Di's

Court During the Han Dynasty

Emperor Wu Di, named Liu Che, was a ruler who was eager to make progress. His civilian administration and military exploits were illustrious. During his rule he established Yue Fu — the office in charge of music — and ordered the performance of the "Hundred Entertainments." He sent Zhang Qian as an envoy to the Western Regions and opened the famous "Silk Road". He promoted economic and cultural exchange between the East and the West, and used acrobatics as a form of diplomacy to meet the needs of certain political conditions. In the spring of the third year of the Yuanfeng reign (108 B.C.), according to the *Records of the Historian*, Emperor Wu Di held grand feasts in honour of the envoys of different countries. He set up "pools of wine and forests of meat" in the capital, Chang'an, in order to show off the prosperity of the Han Dynasty. Along with the banquets, grand performances of the "Hundred Entertainments" were presented, called "a spectacle of Horn Butting Games". This was China's first grand acrobatic performance at the imperial court, and also the first time in Chinese history that acrobatic art was presented for diplomatic purposes. It was a performance of far-reaching significance, held in Pingleguan in Chang'an.

It is reported that the viewing stand occupied a commanding position, with its seats partitioned by gorgeous drapery. The emperor watched the performances, leaning against a jade teapoy and with a quilt of em-

erald colour on his lap. The ministers and foreign guests viewed the artistic performance while feasting. The commoners also came from as far as 150 kilometres away to watch the performances.

The performances comprised "Horn Butting Games" on a grand scale, including wrestling, weight-lifting, juggling swords, juggling balls and fighting animals. There were also "Marvellous Illusions", namely, the presentation of a fairyland based on ancient mythical stories. This took the form of clouds rising and snow flying, mists and fogs, accompanied by the singing and dancing of fairy maidens and goddesses. Such performances were similar to magic, but also resembled drama and song and dance shows. The third part consisted of a display of "strange creatures", the rare birds and animals from the preserve of Emperor Wu Di.

Although mainly Chinese items were presented at this performance, foreign artists also performed many acrobatic items, giving it the rich flavour of the Western Regions. There were the magic tricks of the Romans including "Swallowing a Knife", "Spitting Fire", "Planting Melons", "Planting Trees", "Slaughtering People", "Killing Horses" and "Tying and Untying Oneself" (Figure 11). Other items included "Feats on a Pole" by Burmese and "Snake Trickery" by Indians (Figures 12 & 13).

This international acrobatic festival is said to have achieved the effect which Emeror Wu Di of Han had expected. The

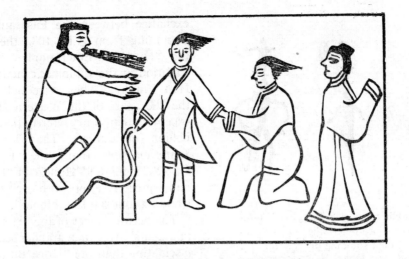

11. Stone carving in a Han Dynasty tomb in Jiaxiang, Shandong Province, showing performers spitting fire and brandishing a whip (copy).

12. Stone carvings in a Han Dynasty Tomb in Jiaxiang, Shandong Province, showing performers sporting with snakes (copy).

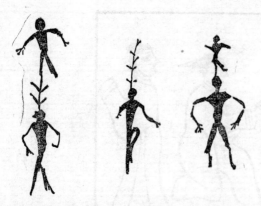

13. Ancient cliff carvings in Cangyuan County, Yunnan Province describing pole balancing and an acrobat standing on the tip of a pole balanced on another performer's forehead (cpoy).

performances showed the bravery, intelligence and enthusiasm of the Chinese people and the wealth and power of the country. They impressed the foreign guests and achieved the diplomatic goal of attracting the states of the Western Regions to establish friendly ties and join efforts with the Han Dynasty to tackle the powerful enemy — the Xiongnus. They also served as a prelude to later cultural exchange between the East and the West. Beginning from A.D. 108, the festival of the "Hundred Entertainments" became a tradition in the diplomatic activities of the Han Empire. They were held throughout the 200 years of the Western Han Dynasty except for temporary interruptions due to rebellion or famine. The *Records of the Historian* tells that "the 'Horn Butting Games', magic and 'Hundred Entertainments' had a greater variety with each passing year, standing out in full bloom".

The performances of the "Hundred Entertainments" were on a grander scale and more fascinating than the "Horn Butting Games" during the time of Emperor Wu Di. In the *Rhyme-Prose on the Western Capital*, Zhang Heng, a scientist and man of letters who lived during the Eastern Han Dynasty, wrote a detailed account of the performances. It is from Zhang Heng that we learn of the encouragement of acrobatics by the imperial court, the exchange between Chinese and foreign artists, and the professional training received by the performers which resulted in great progress in acrobatics during the Han Dynasty.

Feature-Length Magic — "Fish-Dragon Show"

"Fish-Dragon Show" was the earliest recorded item of Chinese magic which had a fairly comprehensive form. It was also one of the representative works of court acrobatics during the Han Dynasty. Subsequent dynasties often used "Fish-Dragon Show" to refer to acrobatics or even the "Hundred Entertainments" as a whole.

There is a description of this feature-length magic show which used stage properties made of silks in *Rhyme-Prose on the Western Capital* written by Zhang Heng. It describes how, from the back of an 250-metre-long dragon, there suddenly appears a mystic mountain. There are numerous and varied parts to this ingenious "Fish-Dragon Show". First, an auspicious animal named "Sarira" appears, frolics in the courtyard, and then jumps into a pond. The animal, in a watery spray, suddenly becomes a flatfish. The fish swims and raises its head to spray water, making the scene hazy. The flatfish then suddenly turns into a dazzling yellow dragon, 25 metres long, which plays around out of the water, in the sunshine. This was, reportedly, a magnificent and cleverly conceived magic show (Figure 14).

鯉魚化鰲式

14. "Fish Show" — Rubbing of a stone carving in a Han Dynasty tomb in Yinan, Shandong Province.

"Fish-Dragon Show" was said to have been warmly received by the people of several dynasties subsequent to the Han Dynasty. Historical records show that traces of this performance could still be found among the folk entertainments at the time of the Wei (A.D. 220-265), Jin (A.D. 265-420), Sui (A.D. 581-618) and Tang dynasties, and down to the Qing Dynasty (A.D. 1644-1911). *E Huan Xu Bian* (*Sequel to Magic*) written in the Qing Dynasty called this performance "Carp Turning into Dragon" (Figure 15). It was basically the same as the "Fish-Dragon Show" of the Han Dynasty but on a much smaller scale, and not necessarily performed with the use of water.

再變鰲魚化龍式

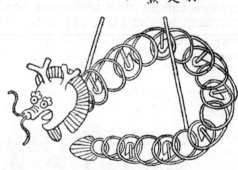

15. Two pictures of "Carp Turning into Dragon" from the book *E Huan Xu Bian* (*Sequel to Magic*) of the Qing Dynasty.

The Development of Handstands

Chinese acrobats call backward waist-bending, leg kicking, somersaults and handstands the essential skills. Each acrobat must have a good command of these four gymnastic skills, with the handstand being the most important technique. Initiated very early, it was widely practised by acrobats across the country. During the Han Dynasty the skill of performing handstands was constantly being improved.

Pottery figurines from the Western Han Dynasty, dug up in Shandong, depict two acrobats in the handstand position — two hands on the ground and two feet up in the air. This is the most basic and most frequently seen handstand position. In contrast, figurines on a pottery dressing case unearthed from the Eastern Han Dynasty present a more skilful handstand performance (Figures 16 & 17), that of two acrobats doing handstands on the edge of a jar. Not only was this more difficult than performing handstands on the ground, but to add to the complexity of skill, a third acrobat was doing a handstand on the two acrobats who were in the upside down position. The complexity in the development of handstands can be seen from the two unearthed antiques, each from a different dynasty.

16. Handstands with one performer on top of another in a picture of feasting and entertainments on a Han Dynasty stone carving (copy).

17. Handstands on drums — Rubbing of a stone carving in a Han Dynasty tomb in Jining, Shandong Province.

The performance of a handstand on the topmost of several small tables, one stacked precipitously on top of another has been found illustrated on brick reliefs excavated in Sichuan (Figure 18). This was called "Five Tables from Partava", and the name suggests that it might have blended the traditional "handstand" with a new form introduced from the Western Regions. Moving the handstand from the ground into the air called for greater skill. The static stance was further developed into a handstand on the top of a high pole on a carriage pulled by galloping horses (Figure 19). This further increas-

18. Brick reliefs of the Han Dynasty showing handstand on tables piled one on top of the other, juggling balls and the "Hundred Entertainments".

19. Handstand on a platform rising high above a carriage — Rubbing of a stone carving in a Han Dynasty tomb in Yinan, Shandong Province.

ed the difficulty of the handstand, since it was very difficult to balance the human body on a high, shaking pole.

In addition to the handstand, supported by two hands, the performance of a handstand on a single hand (Figure 20) was discovered illustrated on a stone sculpture in Henan Province. From the constant variations and innovations in handstand positions, we can see the signs of development in Han Dynasty acrobatics.

20. Single-handed handstand — Rubbing of a stone carving in a Han Dynasty tomb in Nanyang, Henan Province.

Pictorial Records of the Eastern Han Dynasty "Hundred Entertainments"

A picture of the "Hundred Entertainments" on a stone carving discovered in a Han Dynasty tomb in Beizhai Village, Yinan County, Shandong Province, in 1954 depicts vividly, and in fine detail, a lively acrobatic performance of the Eastern Han Dynasty (Figure 21).

The carving pictures 54 performers coordinating with one another in perfect harmony and forming a vivacious ensemble. First is "Juggling Swords", one of the most popular items of juggling with the hands during the Han Dynasty (Figure 22). An old artist, with his hair and beard fluttering, is juggling four short swords with apparent rapt attention. When exerting his strength he is in a slightly squatting posture and appears to act with natural grace. Beside his feet are five balls which he has apparently just juggled. Recorded materials tell us that small holes have been drilled into the balls and when thrown into the air they ring with a melodious whistle due to the vibration of the air, hence they are called "Ball Bell". By the side of this acrobat can be seen a middle-aged male performer with his

21. "Picture of the Hundred Entertainments" — Rubbing of a stone carving in a Han Dynasty tomb in Yi'nan,' Shandong Province.

22. "Juggling Swords" — Detail one of the "Picture of the Hundred Entertainments".

23. "Pole Balancing" — Detail two of the "Picture of the Hundred Entertainments".

upper body naked, whose arms appear as strong as the limbs of a tiger and whose waist looks like that of a bear. He balances a cross-shaped long pole on his forehead and three children are spinning, one lying prostrate on the tip of the pole and the other two suspended by their feet from a horizontal bar (Figure 23). This was a famous new acrobatic act of the Han Dynasty called "Climbing the Long Pole from Dulu" (Dulu was a small state in the Western Regions whose acrobats were famed for agility). This item assimilated the best features of acrobatic skill which had been introduced from Dulu along the "Silk Road". Below can be seen a male performer in a loose-fitting robe with long sleeves, dancing with knees bent and the sash of his robe fluttering. On his right seven tray-shaped drums are arranged in a row. Called the "Seven Tray Dance", this was the most popular acrobatic dance of that time (Figure 24).

A large orchestra is pictured behind this acrobatic performance. In the rear are musicians playing percussion instruments, striking bells and beating drums. One musician thumps a Jian drum with two mallets decorated with feathers and tassels. Another musician, holding a wooden mallet suspended from a large beam, appears to rhythmically strike a huge bell hung on a wooden frame. A third musician sitting in a solemn posture and wearing a top hat, is shown striking a chime stone. Fourteen musicians perform musical accompaniment, seated in three rows. In the front row are female drummers, one of them conducting the orchestra. The vertical bamboo flute is the main wind instrument in the middle row, and ancient lutes and reed pipes are placed in the rear row.

— 23 —

24. "Seven Tray Dance" — Detail three of the "Picture of the Hundred Entertainments".

A breath-taking rope walking act is shown being performed behind the orchestra (Figure 25). A long rope is suspended between two tripods, with knives and swords placed underneath the rope. Three women are performing simultaneously on the rope. On each side is a performer with a short flag in her hands, walking towards the middle. The acrobat in the middle of the rope is performing a handstand with her feet spread upward and her waist bending like a swallow fanning its wings. The superb skill of balancing is depicted in this illustration.

The next performance to be seen is an

25. "Handstand on a Rope" — Detail four of the "Picture of the Hundred Entertainments".

26. "Dragon Masquerade Show" — Detail five of the
"Picture of the Hundred Entertainments".

"Animal Masquerade Show", popular during the time of the Han Dynasty. A dragon-shaped horse carrying a painting, which symbolizes good luck, appears on the scene (Figure 26). The horse is dressed up as a dragon with two horns and a huge mouth and is covered all over with scales. A scroll painting is carried on horseback, and on the upper side stands a child playing with a feather canopy and a long pendant. Led by a rattle-drum and a sectional whip, the dragon-horse marches ahead in what appears to be hurried steps, while the child with a broad smile stands at ease on the galloping horse. In the rear people carry a giant fish made of coloured silks. Three performers swinging long-handled, small rattle-drums are teasing the horse. This ancient scene was called "Fish-Dragon Show".

A leopard masquerade follows: Someone in the skin of a leopard, its mouth in a grin, its eyes opened wide, crouches and leaps while holding a flag. A child, in a feathered cape, with hands on the ground and legs in the air, is playing with the leopard in what appears to be a naive and charming manner (Figure 27). This resembles a little boy playing with a lion in the present-day "Lion Dance".

Another performance is that of a person masquerading as a big bird, with its crest erect and wings spread. It looks like a phoenix with long feathers and has a ribbon with tassels hanging down under its jaw. Little bells are attached to its tail, and exposed are a pair of human feet. In front of the bird is a man wearing a garment made of flower petals and holding a Chinese parasol tree in his hand, signifying that a parasol tree is attracting the phoenix (Figure 28). This series of bird-or-animal masquerade shows were obviously drawn from ancient Chinese mythological stories in which the imitation of gods, goddesses and rare birds and animals in fairyland symbolized good luck, peace and happiness.

The last part of the carving portrays a magnificent and lively circus (Figures 29 & 30). Two fine horses appear to be galloping towards each other with their heads high and their tails curled. Their hooves are in the air to signify they are in motion. On the left, on horseback, stands a young woman with ribbons tied in her hair and wearing a short skirt. She is holding a halberd in her left hand and a long rope in her right hand, re-

27. "Leopard Masquerade Show" — Detail six of the
"Picture of the Hundred Entertainments".

Animal Masquerade — ... the time of the Han Dynasty ... shaped horse carrying a painting, when sym- balizes good luck, appears on the scene (Figure 26). The horse is dressed up as a dragon with two horns and a huge mouth and is covered all over with scales. A second painting is carried on horseback, and on the upper side stands a child playing with a feather canopy and ... rattle-drum and a various ... horse matches good ...

... masquerade at cere- ... for the rear people ... coloured silks. The ... long-handled spear ... the horse. Thus a ... Leopard Drum in Sho- ... Leopard masquer- on the skin of a leopard ... its eyes opened w- ... the white holding a flute ... come, with hands on the ... ground is playing with the leop- ... seems to be a native and charming manner ... (Figure 27). This resembles little boys play- ... ing with a lion in the present-day Lion ...

... masquerading as a big bird, with its crest erect and ... wings spread. It looks like a phoenix with long feathers and has a ribbon with tassels hanging down under its jaw. Little bells are attached to its tail, and except- ed are a pair of human feet. In front of the bird is a man wearing a garment made of ... and holding a Chinese parasol ... ing, that a parasol ... els (Figure 28). ... animal masquerade ... awn from ancient ... ings in which the ... tures and rare birds ... symbolized good ...

... tearing, portrays a ... tions (Figure 29 & ... ear to be galloping ... her hands high and ... bow-strings are in the ... ... in motion. On the left, ... stands a young woman, well ... ... ribbon, clad in her hair and wearing a short ... ... skirt. She is holding something in her left ... ... hand and a long rope in her right hand, tos- ...

28. "Bird Show" — Detail seven of the "Picture
of the Hundred Entertainments".

— 26 —

29. "Display on Horseback" Detail eight of the "Picture of the Handred Entertainments".

30. Grabbing at the mane to leap onto the horse's back — Detail nine of the "Picture of the Hundred Entertainments.

sembling the "Swinging Meteors" in today's acrobatics. On the right is a man holding a hook in one hand and gripping the horse's mane in the other, as if ready to leap onto the horse's back with lightning speed. Below are three horses decked out to look like dragons; they are galloping abreast and pulling a performance chariot. On the chariot are a Jian drum and two long poles, each with a small platform on top. Young performers are doing backward waist-bending and handstands on the platforms. To accompany these exciting acrobatic skills, musicians in and outside the chariot are playing flutes and reed pipes and beating drums.

This grand acrobatic performance of the Eastern Han Dynasty dating back 1,800 years, was carved with simple lines. It can be seen from the carving that this acrobatic troupe had a complete assortment of performers. The 23 artists, male and female, old and young, each shows his or her own special skill. They appear to be vying with one another. The artists display extraordinary skill. The male dancers present graceful but vigorous dancing movements, and the leopard duet is shown doing leaps, bounces and somersaults. The boy on the dragon looks natural and unrestrained, the girl on horseback seems ready to make quick, resolute movements, and the rope-walking performers appear calm and steady. It can be interpreted that the Han Dynasty artists had a warm love for acrobatics and a fidelity to the art.

The carving portrays a very colourful performance, displaying a great variety of skills and entertainments and consisting of juggling with the hands or feet, handstands, somersaults, feats in the air, masquerade shows, circuses, performances on horse-drawn chariots, gymnastic feats, dancing and conjury. It is varied and superb in execution.

As can be seen from the stone carving, Han Dynasty acrobatics gave meticulous care to artistic form. Each part of the performance utilized exquisite costumes and stage properties, giving the whole scene a romantic flavour. For example, there are long dresses suitable for showing graceful figures and short jackets fit for galloping on horseback and climbing high; there were also skirts resembling flower petals, feather capes and swallow-tailed coats. Even horses were dressed up to look like dragons. All these attractive costumes were closely linked with the content of the performance. Set off by the musical accompaniment of a 27-member orchestra, the performance must have been, indeed, marvellous in sound, colour and artistry.

Reviewing the acrobatic art of the Han Dynasty, we can see that it had already blossomed by that time. Although acrobatic art and other art forms were grouped together as the "Hundred Entertainments", it had its own performances which were fairly spectacular, and not merely a display of gymnastic skills. The performance and the stage properties, costumes and music set off one another. Superb skills were blended with beauty of imagery colour, tempo and rhythm. What is more important, was that the acrobatic art of various states in the Western Regions began to infiltrate into the intrinsic acrobatic performances of the Chinese nation, blazing the trail for Chinese acrobatics to diversify, and contributing to the great variety in Chinese acrobatics.

Han Dynasty acrobatics represented an important stage in the history of Chinese acrobatics, laying a solid foundation for the development of Chinese acrobatic art over the past 2,000 years.

3. Developing in the Midst of Chaos
(A.D. 220-581)

When the regime of the Eastern Han Dynasty suffered a fatal blow from the nationwide uprising of the Yellow Turbans peasant army, it was shaken to its foundations. This brought about the disintegration of the Eastern Han empire. Warlords established independent regimes, relying on the strength of their own troops. The country was divided into three parts. Cao Cao laid the foundation for the establishment of the Kingdom of Wei. Cao Pi, his son, got rid of the puppet emperor of the Eastern Han empire and proclaimed the formation of the new kingdom with himself as emperor, ruling the northern region. Sun Quan's Kingdom of Wu occupied the middle and lower reaches of the Yangtze River. Liu Bei declared himself emperor, occupying Sichuan Province, and adopted the old dynastic title of Han, but history calls the regime the Kingdom of Shu. This period was known to history as the Three Kingdoms (A.D. 220 - 265).

In A.D. 265 Sima Yan superseded the Kingdom of Wei and established the Western Jin Dynasty (A.D. 265-316). He conquered the kingdoms of Wu and Shu and unified China. Shortly afterwards, relentless struggles for power and internecine wars broke out among members of the royal house of the Western Jin Dynasty.

The nobles of the five nomadic minority tribes inhabiting the northern region came with their troops into the interior and ruled the Central Plains. One state after another was established on the ruins of its predecessor, in a series of short-lived regimes. This period is known in Chinese history as that of the Sixteen States. Owing to frequent wars in the north, the ruler of the Western Jin Dynasty had to flee to the south and founded the Eastern Jin Dynasty. (A.D. 317-420). In 420 Liu Yu, a general of the Eastern Jin Dynasty, superseded Jin and proclaimed the inauguration of the Song Dynasty. South China went through the rule of four dynasties: Song, Qi, Liang and Chen. These became known as the Southern Dynasties (A.D. 420-589).

Meanwhile, the Toba branch of the Xianbei people in the north gradually eliminated other states, unified almost the whole of northern China and established the Northern Wei Dynasty. Later, the Northern Wei Dynasty disintegrated and the Eastern Wei and the Western Wei dynasties came into being. A short time afterwards, the Eastern Wei and the Western Wei dynasties were superseded by the Northern Qi and the Northern Zhou dynasties. The Northern Zhou Dynasty eliminated the Northern Qi Dynasty and again unified the north. This period became known as the Northern Dynasties (A.D. 386-581). This approximately 400-year period is known as "the Wei, Jin and Southern and Northern Dynasties" in Chinese history.

The 400-year-long tangled warfare in the

Wei, Jin and Southern and Northern Dynasties caused great damage to social economy. The people were constantly harassed by wars and worked hard in a life-or-death struggle. Natural and man-made calamities alternated and there was utter desolation. Hungry people swarmed the country and bodies of the starved were strewn everywhere. Under such circumstances literature and art suffered from many adversities. But acrobatic art was deeply rooted among the people and could still pass down and was even developed to a certain extent, despite difficulties. This showed its tenacity.

Social chaos brought new features to acrobatics. During brutal war conditions it was, of course, difficult for acrobats to present such grand performances as during the Han Dynasty. But to be itinerant performers in twos and threes or even roaming and performing alone, was more convenient than performing other art forms. Therefore, in the Wei, Jin and Southern and Northern Dynasties, folk acrobatic performances spread widely north and south of the Yangtze River. The "Biography of Empress Zhen" in *San Guo Zhi* (*History of the Three Kingdoms*) written by Chen Shou of the Western Jin; *Rhyme-Prose on Apes and Monkeys*, an elaborate descriptive prose written by Fu Xuan, a man of letters in the Western Jin; and *Sou Shen Ji* (*Records of Spirits*), a collection of short stories about gods and supernatural beings, record how artists gave itinerant performances of acrobatics, circuses and magic shows. Composed of short acts, and without language or geographical barrier, acrobatic performances were well adapted to every circumstance.

Warfare brought about the merging of nationalities and made it possible for extensive art exchange between different nationalities. In the course of the immigration of the five northern Hu tribes and the establishment of the Sixteen States to rule the Central Plains, quite a number of minority nationalities came into the interior and inevitably brought with them their own art. Both the Kucha dance introduced from Kucha (Present-day Kuqa in Xinjiang) and Kashgar (present-day Kashi and Shule in Xinjiang), and the dance of the Western Regions from Gansu Province contained a certain number of acrobatic items. For instance, the "Lion Dance", "Pole Balancing", "Monkey Jockey Shows" and "Juggling Five Kinds of Weapons" all sprung up at this time. The merging of nationalities enriched acrobatic art.

Most rulers in troubled times sought pleasure and amusement. To meet the needs of their extravagant life and to present a false picture of peace and prosperity, they often summoned acrobats and performers of the "Hundred Entertainments" into the palace. The Northern Wei (A.D. 386-534), the Eastern Wei (A.D. 534-550), the Northern Qi (A.D. 550-577), the Northern Zhou (A.D. 557-581) and the Southern Dynasties had all introduced something new to acrobatics and to the "Hundred Entertainments". This increased the number and improved the quality of acrobatic items.

The "Section of Music" in *Sui Shu* (*History of the Sui Dynasty*) records that in the Wuping reign (A.D. 570-575) of Gao Wei, Emperor Houzhu of the Northern Qi Dynasty, there were about 100 fantastic items such as "Fish-Dragon Show", "Dwarfs", "Mountain Chariots", "Huge Elephants", "Pulling Out of Wells", "Planting Melons", "Killing Horses" and "Skinning Donkeys" which were called the "Hundred Entertainments". This represented only a single region. If we take into account all acrobatic numbers popular in different places in the south and north, they would come up to an enormous number.

"Monkey Jockey Shows" and "Juggling Five Kinds of Weapons"

"Monkey Jockey Shows" and "Juggling Five Kinds of Weapons" may be considered representative works of northern acrobatics in the Southern and Northern Dynasties. "Monkey Jockey Shows" can be traced back to a form of circus show of ancient nomadic tribes. It spread into the Central Plains in the 4th century. It was presented in the following fashion: a performer wearing a sheet of monkey skin to masquerade as a monkey, demonstrated horsemanship on a galloping horse. He stood on the head of the horse, then reaching below its belly, with his feet still in the stirrups, pulled hard at the horse's tail and quickly leapt onto the horse's back. . . . Showing extraordinary agility, he could rival a monkey.

The performance of "Monkey Jockey Shows" is described in *Tai Ping Huan Yu Ji* (*Taiping Geographical Record*) completed in the Taipingxingguo reign (A.D. 976-983). The performer could stand with one foot on horseback and bend his other leg to serve as

the desk and, in an unsteady, swaying posture, give a swift calligraphy demonstration. The "Monkey Jockey Show", both in acrobatic difficulty and in artistic treatment, developed a new and distinctive style (Figures 31, 32 & 33).

The above-mentioned "Monkey Jockey Show" was an item put on by a performer dressed up as a monkey. But there are also traces of real monkey jockey shows which can be found from ancient times. From the Tang Dynasty are two lines of poetry,

A brave warrior's aspirations have not come true.
Just like a monkey rides on dog back.

Tai Ping Guang Ji (*Records of the Taiping Era*), a collection of ancient notes and short stories completed in the Taipingxingguo reign, records that "a monkey on dog back impersonates a general", explaining that in ancient times there were animal shows in which a monkey rode on ox back or on dog

31. "Circus Show: — Rubbing of a stone carving in the Confucian Temple in Linzi, Shandong Province.

back. There still exists a show in which a monkey on sheep back jumps through hoops of fire.'

"Juggling Five Kinds of Weapons" appeared in the early period of the Northern Wei Dynasty. "*Wei Shu (History of the Northern Wei Dynasty)*, written in the style of biographies by Wei Shou of the Northern Qi Dynasty, records: "Emperor Dao Wu of the Later Wei Dynasty in the winter of the seventh year of the Tianxing reign [A.D. 404] issued an imperial edict urging the official in charge of music and entertainments to improve upon drums and wind instruments, enrich the 'Hundred Entertainments' and create the item of 'Juggling with Five Kinds of Weapons'." The latter item was specially mentioned in the enrichment of the "Hundred Entertainments", which testifies to the importance of this item. The five kinds of weapons were *ge* (dagger-axe), *mao* (spear), *ji* (halberd), *jian* (sword) and *gong* (bow) of ancient China. These weapons were reportedly first made of metal by Chi

You in ancient times. In the passages above, we already mentioned that "Horn Butting Games" were developed from "Chi You's Games" and were also a sport which had evolved from bare-handed wrestling. "Juggling Five Kinds of Weapons" combined "Horn Butting Games" with the use of weapons. It might possibly have been another branch of ancient "Chi You's Games" which had long been popular in northern nomadic areas. Only in the Wei and Jin dynasties was it brought to the Central Plains by some minority nationalities. It combined the display of weapons with acrobatic skills and blazed a new trail for the development of acrobatics. "Juggling Halberds" and

32. "Tiger Fight" — Rubbing of a stone carving in a Han Dynasty tomb in Nanyang, Henan Province.

33. "Circus Show" — Rubbing of a stone carving in a Han Dynasty tomb in Dengfeng, Shandong Province.

"Knife Throwing", warmly appreciated by audiences of that time, and "Flying Tridents", "Javelin Throw" and "Five-Tiger Clubs"--items enjoying great popularity in subsequent dynasties — were all derived from "Juggling Five Kinds of Weapons". Martial arts were encouraged as was the use of weapons in acrobatics. This was characteristic of the then turbulent times, when there were frequent wars.

Graceful Acrobatics of the South

After the Eastern Jin Dynasty established its capital in Jiankang (present-day Nanjing in Jiangsu Province), the political centre of the Han nationality moved to the south. One-eighth of the people on the Central Plains fled south and the traditional acrobatics popular in that region also went south of the Yangtze and blended with the local art. Elegant, graceful acrobatics of the south came into being. This and the warm, unrestrained style of northern acrobatics each had its own good features.

The acrobatics of the south carried on the tradition of Han Dynasty acrobatics. So the traditional items such as "Rope Walking", "Tripod Lifting" and "Conjuring" were often put on in the Yangtze valley. A number of new, elegant and ingenious items also appeared. For instance, the performance of turning somersaults, first mentioned in written records in the Liang Dynasty (A.D. 502-557) of the Southern Dynasties, further developed into turning somersaults on a table. This was more difficult than turning somersaults on the ground since there was a smaller surface for movements. Turning somersaults on stilts was also developed, which presented an acrobatic skill quite different from the other two items. Meanwhile, animal shows such as monkey shows and mouse shows also became very popular.

Scenery made of coloured silks were richly tinged with the characteristics of southern China. They were evolved from feature-length magic shows such as "Fish-Dragon Shows" popular during the Han Dynasty. Scenery made of coloured silks blended magic and masquerade into an artistic whole. Examples of this were the ingenious performance "Phoenix Delivering a Message", and the magnificent "Spectacle of Tiantai Mountain".

According to records in the "Music Section" of Qi Shu (History of the Qi Dynasty) written in the style of biographies by Xiao Zixian of the Liang Dynasty, "Phoenix Delivering a Message" was a performance presented in court ceremonies. Whenever the court held a grand ceremony, the auspicious phoenix gently flew down from the sky, holding a scroll of congratulatory message in its beak. A courtier took it and read it in front of the officials so as to extend congratulations to the emperor. This was different from the Han Dynasty item when a performer masquerading as the phoenix walked on the ground. Now the phoenix could hold a congratulatory message in its beak and fly up and down in the palace. From the written description, one can visualize the ingenious design and exquisite craftsmanship. The "Spectacle of Tiantai Mountain" was a feature-length magic show in which a Taoist priest opened up a stone wall and suddenly there appeared a scene of fairyland, exotic in colour and involving complicated changes. These two performances illustrate that the acrobatic and magic items at that time were more refined and mature than those at the time of the Han Dynasty.

Feats Aloft in a Great Variety of Styles

Traditional feats on poles progressed and developed a variety of styles during the Wei, Jin and Southern and Northern Dynasties. *Yue Shu* (*The Book of Music*), a treatise on music written by Chen Yang of the Song Dynasty in 1101, describes an outstanding programme, listing items of entertainment in the sequence of their presentation at the lunar New Year in the sixth century. Among the 49 items there were described as many as nine feats on poles. One of these was an energetic performance of "A Hundred Tigers on a Pole"; others included "Parasol on a Pole", which presented a human pyramid on pole, "Feats on a Table", in which acrobats performed difficult skills on a table, "Feats on a Wheel," in which there was innovative use of stage properties, and "Monkey Feats on a Pole" in which performers masqueraded as monkeys and imitated their movements. There were many descriptions of climbing up poles and balancing a pole on the head or forehead, and each required its own special skill. These feats on poles showed advancement in skill when compared with "Midget Climbing a Pole" and "Climbing the Long Pole from Dulu" from the preceding dynasties.

Varied and colourful items of pole balancing during the Southern and Northern Dynasties spread to the Central Plains, because of the merging of various nationality groups. There are many historical records explaining the sequence of this development. For instance, the "Pole Balancing of Northern Hu Tribes" used to be a skill performed only by people of the Western Regions but was brought to southern China by prisoners of war.

Ye Zhong Ji (*Notes on the City of Ye*), written by Lu Hui of the Eastern Jin Dynasty (317-420), describes many special pole balancing feats which were performed during feasting and entertainments at the imperial court in the period of the Sixteen States created by the five northern Hu tribes. For example, in the description of "Pole on Forehead", a pole was placed on the forehead of a performer and an acrobat on the tip of the pole whirled to and fro like a flying bird

34 a. Acrobatic performance carved on a stone monument of the Northern Wei Dynasty (rubbing).

(Figures 34 a-b).

"Pole on Teeth" was an item in which a pole was placed upright on the teeth of an acrobat who used the strength of his jaw to support the weight of a pole and another acrobat. In the performance of "Pole on a Carriage", a wooden pole more than seven metres high was hoisted on the top of a carriage. A horizontal piece of wood was placed on the tip of the pole, and on it sat two acrobatics, one on each end, performing handstands and the movements of a flying bird.

In a famous mural in the Dunhuang Caves in Gansu Province, there is a picture of an acrobatic performance from the Northern Wei Dynasty (386-581) of "Pole on Abdomen". It shows an acrobat bending his body backward, making it look like a bridge, and with a long pole erected on his abdomen. Anoth-er acrobat is on the tip of the pole, also doing backward waist-bending. With his hands and feet on the ground, the acrobat below controlled his focus entirely through the sense of the muscles of his abdomen. This, indeed, was far from easy (Figure 35).

The Sixteen States created by the five northern Hu tribes and the Northern Wei Dynasty were political powers established by minority nationalities. The gradual advancement of acrobatics in the Wei, Jin and Southern and Nothern Dynasties is explained by the fact that the people of various nationalities pooled their efforts. This led to the creation of a truly Chinese acrobatic form which utilized the wisdom and talent of the many nationality groups of China.

34 b. Detail of the acrobatic performance carved on the stone monument, from the Northern Wei Dynasty (copy).

35. Copy of a picture of pole balancing and walking on stilts on the murals of the Wei and Jin dynasties in Dunhuang, Gansu Province.

New Developments in the Art of Magic

During the Wei, Jin and Southern and Northern Dynasties there were frequent wars and oppressive political conditions. The corrupt and decadent rulers scrambled for power and wealth. The commoners, in the abyss of their miseries, usually pinned their hopes on religion and the concept of a life after death. Posing as persons of high morals, the rulers advocated Taoism and Buddhism. They built temples and monasteries and opened up grottoes emphasizing religion, which left deep imprints on the literature and art of that time.

During the period of its initiation, acrobatic art was in some ways related to religious sacrificial ceremonies, but the ties became closer at this time. To make people believe in their supernatural powers, Buddhist and Taoist priests often performed magic tricks to heighten the atmosphere and deceive the people. Although they flatly denied they were performing conjury, the "Supernatural Art" they demonstrated consisted of genuine conjuring tricks. Under the guise of religion some priests claimed to be Bodhisattvas, gods or goddesses. The story of "Zuo Ci Fools Cao Cao" popular during the period of the Three Kingdoms is a typical example of this activity (Figure 36).

According to this story from *Hou Han Shu* (*History of the Later Han Dnyasty*) there was a man named Zuo Ci who claimed to be good at supernatural art. One day Cao Cao invited him and many other guests to a grand banquet. When it was close to the time for the feast, Cao Cao said apologetically to all the guests, "Today many honourable friends have come here for a gathering and I've prepared some wines to drink and food to eat, but I am sorry I don't have perch from the Songjiang River to serve you". Zuo Ci

36. Zuo Ci throwing a wine goblet (magic show) — a woodcut from the Qing Dynasty.

responded to this, saying, "I'm able to solve this problem." He asked the attendants to get a bronze basin and fill it with clear water. He then tied bait onto a bamboo rod and began to fish in the basin, soon fishing up a perch. Cao Cao and all the guests present were astonished. Cao Cao then said, "One fish doesn't suffice to entertain so many guests. Can you fish up several?" Zuo Ci again put the fishing rod into the water after replacing the bait. A short while later, he fished up another perch and then several more, all fresh fish and more than a metre long. Cao Cao at once bade the chef to cook the perches for the feast. Giving Zuo Ci another challenge, he said, "To cook this perch one needs purple sprout ginger from Sichuan as a condiment, but I am afraid we can't get it." Zuo Ci realized that Cao Cao was testing his ability, and so replied confidently "If you need ginger I can produce it, too." He then conjured up many pieces of palatable ginger from Sichuan which made people believe him to be a god.

Some time later, Cao Cao, escorted by more than 100 officials and attendants, went on an excursion. They brought along much wine and food planning to have a sumptuous picnic. Zuo Ci was among the company. He brought with him only a litre of wine and half a kilogramme of dried meat. Drinking and eating alone in a leisurely and contented manner, he invited others to join him. Although many of them ate and drank their fill, Zuo Ci still had wine and meat left over. Cao Cao thought it strange and wondered how so many people could eat and drink their fill when there was only a litre of wine and half a kilogramme of dried meat. He learned that Zuo Ci had stealthily managed to get all the wine and dishes which had been prepared by Cao Cao and used them to feed the people, and that's why he did not exhaust his own supply of wine and meat. Cao Cao had always thought himself more clever than

others, but he was fooled by Zuo Ci. At this he was so enraged that he declared that he would put Zuo Ci to death. The story ends by having Zuo Ci escape by bumping himself against a wall and vanishing.

If we remove the mysticism from this vivid anecdote, we can see that what Zuo Ci performed were merely conjuring tricks. Chinese folk artists today often perform similar tricks, including "The Vanished Cup", "Fishing with an Empty Rod", "Planting Ginger in a Golden Pot", "Drawing Wine Unexhausted" and "Vanishing Act".

The performance of magic tricks were original and full of novelty at that time. They differed from those longer performances such as "Fish-Dragon Show" which people could see used false fish and animals, or from those breathtaking performances of horror such as "Swallowing a Knife" or "Spitting Fire". The performance of magic tricks used things on hand in daily life as stage properties and were performed in the midst of the spectators. The emergence of these tricks marked a new level of development attained by Chinese magic. No matter what Zuo Ci's purpose was in creating these items, they propelled forward the development of Chinese magic and blazed a new trail for the Chinese style of performing short magic tricks.

The Rise of Temple Fairs

Acrobatics and magic were also used in China to spread the doctrines of Buddhism during the Southern and Northern Dynasties. The rulers made great efforts to foster this religion and it soon became prevalent. There were many monks and nuns and a great number of temples and monasteries. According to *Luo Yang Qie Lan Ji* (*Records of Buddhist Temples in Luoyang*) written by Yang Xuanzhi of the Northern Wei Dynasty, there were several hundred temples and monasteries

in Luoyang alone. Buddhist monks often made use of temple fairs to win over devotees. Apart from expounding scriptures and Buddhist teachings, the temple fairs usually presented entertainment with a religious flavour. Nominally they were intended for worshipping Buddhas and Bodhisattvas but in actuality they were more in the nature of amusement. The temple fairs provided spots for the display of acrobatics and the "Hundred Entertainments" which, in their turn, attracted visitors to the temple fairs and enhanced their mystic and lively atmosphere.

Another form of acrobatic performance related to Buddhism was called the Strolling Procession. On the occasion of the birthday of Sakyamuni on the eighth day of the fourth lunar month, Buddhists held a strolling procession on the streets, to sprinkle water on the statue of the Buddha. They carried the statue in the procession and gave acrobatic performances. These performances were recorded in the book *Records of Buddhist Temples in Luoyang* by Yang Xuanzhi when the book describes the celebration of the festival in the Longevity Temple. In the grand procession, some devotees carried three-tiered pagoda and a shrine decorated with gold. White elephants carried the solemn Buddha statues, and many acrobatic items were interspersed. For example, an evil-exorcizing lion opened the way in front and acrobats on horseback swallowing kinves, spitting fire, balancing poles on their head and doing rope walking followed behind. When this procession of people showing marvellous skills and in exotic costumes crossed the streets and halted to give performances, the spectators were so numerous that some people were killed in the crowded streets.

Owing to the encouragement of the rulers, grand Buddhist processions superseded primitive sacrificial ceremonies at religious festivals. Such processions were often held during the more than 1,000 year period between the Wei, Jin and Southern and Northern Dynasties and the end of the Qing Dynasty (A.D. 1644-1911). In the course of time, the temple fair became a traditional form of Chinese folk art performance, and its religious flavour vanished.

The rise of temple fairs and strolling processions produced a deep impact on the creation and performance of acrobatics, and the appearance of "Evil-Exorcizing Lion" is an example. The "Lion Dance" was a type of animal masquerade show which had already become prevalent during the Han Dynasty, but there were no records about the "Lion Dance" in the historical books of that dynasty. "Evil-Exorcizing Lion" was created at the same time and opened the way for other acrobatic items. It had its origin in Buddhist legends. It is said in Buddhist scriptures: "When the Buddha first came, 500 lions arrived from the snow mountain and attended on him at the gate. So the lions served as guardians." Consequently, Buddhism regards lions as guardians of safety and a symbol of good luck. The lion is also known as "evil-exorcizer", which means that a lion drives demons and ghosts away. Lions have appeared in many performances, and acrobatic numbers which include lions have spread widely among the Chinese people and have covered a great variety of forms.

At temple fairs and strolling processions there were usually large crowds of people, and the artists performed and walked forward at the same time. Therefore, simple stage properties were required so that spectators could watch such performances from all sides. Compared with the "Hundred Entertainments" presented at feasts, this was more of an art form for the people and was extremely popular. ·

4. A New Upsurge (A.D. 589-907)

If we say that the "Hundred Entertainments" of the Han Dynasty represented the first upsurge in the history of ancient Chinese acrobatics, acrobatics of the Tang Dynasty was the second upsurge.

In A.D. 589, Yang Jian, Emperor Wen Di of the Sui Dynasty (581-618), unified China and ended the chaos of independent regimes in the north and south. He sent the performers of the "Hundred Entertainments" out from the courts of the various former states to perform and earn their livelihood among the people. This promoted the development of folk acrobatics.

After Yang Guang, Emperor Yang Di of the Sui Dynasty, seized the throne in A.D. 604, he again summoned the performers, who had been sent back among the people, to the eastern capital, Luoyang. They were registered as professional performers, and officials were appointed to supervise them. These performers often presented shows at the imperial court. Emperor Yang Di entertained foreign guests with acrobatics and the "Hundred Entertainments" to show off the prosperity and power of the Sui empire and the well-developed culture of the Central Plains.

The "Music Section" in *Sui Shu* (*History of the Sui Dynasty*) records that in the third year of the Daye reign (A.D. 607), a gigantic tent was set up east of the city of Luoyang to entertain the Khan of the Turks. A traditional full-length magic show including "Yellow Dragon Transformation", "Rope Walking", "Feats of Physical Prowess", "Pole Balancing", "Knife Swallowing" and "Spitting Fire" as well as fantastic shows such as "Mountain on a Magic Turtle's Back" (referring to a legendary giant turtle) were performed. Watching such unprecedented performances of countless variations, some of which used stage properties made of coloured silks, the chieftains of the frontier tribes were greatly impressed. This gave much satisfaction to the arrogant and overbearing Yang Guang who had a desire to show off, so he sponsored such performances for many years in succession (Figure 37).

Owing to the requirements of the large-scale performances, there were an increasing number of registered professional performers, totalling tens of thousands. The performers were placed under an office responsible for rites and music. Every year on the lunar New Year's day (the first day of the first lunar month), the envoys of various countries came to extend festival greetings. Beginning on the 15th of the first lunar month the whole of Luoyang city was bustling with festivities. The four-kilometre-long royal street inside the Jianguo Gate was assigned as grounds for the "Hundred Entertainments". The most spectacular performance, held in the sixth year of the Daye reign (A.D. 610) of Emperor Yang Di, was presented by more than 30,000 people, including an 18,000-member orchestra. The open-air theatre in front of the palace gate in Luoyang was 5,000 steps in perimeter. During the performance, the beating of gongs and drums could be clearly heard five kilometres away.

According to the information in poems and essays written at that time, acrobatics accounted for a large proportion of the grand performances. There were brief acts of juggling

37. Picture of Emperor Yang Di of the Sui Dynasty attending the "Hundred Entertainments" — A woodblock print from the Ming Dynasty.

as a connecting link in the history of acrobatics. It concentrated the "Hundred Entertainments" which had been dispersed for a long period in the south and the north, and lay a foundation for the great development of acrobatics at the height of the Tang Dynasty.

The Sui Dynasty fell due to mass uprisings involving millions of peasants. Rising in its place was the Tang Dynasty (A.D. 618-907) whose rulers drew lessons from the fall of the preceding dynasty. The early Tang Dynasty rulers adopted measures to alleviate social contradictions and to facilitate economic development. After exerting vigorous efforts to make the country peaceful and prosperous, the Tang empire thrived economically and became powerful. Envoys came from distant countries to pay homage at the Tang court, and it became the world's most powerful fedual empire of its time.

Economic prosperity brought about the flowering of culture, and there were brilliant achievements in poetry, prose, painting, music and dance. The Qin and Han dynasties could not rival it in these fields. As the Tang empire pursued the diplomatic policy of equality and friendship, foreign envoys, scholars, merchants, monks, artists and students took the "Silk Road" or sailed across the oceans to journey to China. This promoted economic and cultural exchange between China and other countries.

Under those historical conditions, Tang acrobatic art was in full bloom and made striking progress. First, Tang acrobatics assimilated and blended the cream of art from minority nationalities and countries in western Asia and the Roman empire and so its items were more varied, colourful and magnificent. For instance, the animal masquerade show "Lion Dance", called "Taiping Music" at that time, was part of "Kucina Music", one of the "Ten Books of Music" under the office in charge of rites and music. Kucina was the name of a state in the West-

balls or swords, breathtaking circus shows and a great variety of animal masquerade shows. There were also feature-length magic shows. The most outstanding new item in Sui Dynasty acrobatics was a performance of "Two Acrobats Leap to Each Other's Pole". In this item each of two strongmen had a tall pole on his head with a performer on top of the pole. After presenting a variety of feats on the poles, performers on top of the poles would suddenly leap to each other's pole and continue with their performance. This acrobatic skill of exchanging positions on two not very stable long poles appeared in records for the first time and marked a new level in the skill of pole balancing.

The Sui Dynasty lasted for only 37 years. It was a transient period in history but acted ern Regions, located in the area of present-day Kucha County, Xinjiang.

Second, because of the great attention paid to this field by the rulers, acrobats and acrobatic numbers were under government supervision. Thus the performers had fairly stable living conditions and this was helpful to the improvement of acrobatic skills. The Tang music and the "Hundred Entertainments" were divided into two categories. One of them was small in scale with only a few performers who put on shows in halls, and the other was large in scale and with many performers who gave shows in courtyards and on squares. Acrobatics occupied an important position in the second category.

Li Longji, Emperor Xuan Zong (712-756) of the Tang Dynasty, established court offices in charge of teaching, rehearsing and performing music, singing, dancing and the "Hundred Entertainments". These institutions were large in scale. The office in Chang'an alone supervised more than 10,000 performers of music, dance and the "Hundred Entertainments".

After the middle of the Tang Dynasty, the regimes of military governors in different places and of frontier commanders who had power and troops under their command were actually independent. These warlords, imitating the emperor, each brought together performers of acrobatics and the "Hundred Entertainments" and formed troupes to meet the needs of their luxurious and pleasure-seeking life. This helped to develop and expand the ranks of professional performers of acrobatics and the "Hundred Entertainments". But after rising to its height, the Tang Dynasty declined. Court acrobatics gradually fell into neglect and its performers, relieved of the restrictions of the government and the court, returned to performing among the common people.

The development of Tang Dynasty acro-batic art might be divided into four stages: early Tang Dynasty, Tang Dynasty at its height, mid-Tang Dynasty and late Tang Dynasty. During the early Tang Dynasty period the empire was rising politically, economically and culturally. Its acrobatic art was gigantic in scale and unrestrained, reflecting the flourishing atmosphere at the beginning of the dynasty. During the eighth century the political, economic and cultural development of the Tang empire was at its zenith. Its acrobatic art became magnificent and its skills matured, covering a great variety of forms. It was superb in both sound and colour. This reflected the wealthy and prosperous atmosphere of the Tang Dynasty at its height.

The mid-Tang Dynasty period saw the An-Shi Rebellion (the rebellion of military governors An Lushan and Shi Siming), and the Tang empire gradually declined. Acrobatic art lost its characteristic of magnificence and became melancholy and pathetic. A number of court acrobats dispersed and became folk performers which caused the change of artistic style in acrobatics.

During the late Tang Dynasty period, military governors of outlying provinces had independent regimes, eunuchs held power in their hands and officials of different social strata formed rival cliques. The struggle among them for power lasted for decades. The Tang Dynasty weakened and disintegrated. Acrobatics, although still enjoyed by high officials, nobles and frontier military governors, gradually declined, and sensuous performances increased. But a large number of the performances which constituted the wholesome aspects of acrobatic art developed among the people. Later, this was to influence the rise of the townspeople's literature and art in the Song Dynasty (A.D. 960-1279).

Attending Grand Celebrations and Feasts

Celebrations and feasts were popular during the Tang Dynasty, and lavish banquets were prepared at the court to entertain guests on the lunar New Year and for other festivals. Performances of music, dance and acrobatics were presented in the course of feasting and were called "Grand Celebrations and Feasts". The Han Dynasty had already set a precedent for this practice of attending performances of the "Hundred Entertainments" while feasting, but this became more prevalent during Tang Dynasty.

In the capital, Chang'an, and the eastern capital, Luoyang, the court always held celebrations and feasts on the lunar New Year or for the emperor's birthday, to entertain the envoys of various countries, chieftains of different nationalities and civilian and military officials. These grand celebrations and feasts usually lasted several days and nights. For instance, during the reign of Emperor Xuan Zong, in the early half of the eighth century, at every Lantern Festival on the 15th of the first lunar month, the grounds under the Qinzheng Building in Chang'an were decked out with bright flags, and guards in golden armour stood in neat array. Acrobats, musicians and dancers in diverse costumes came in a continuous stream. Some drove small carts and sailed imaginary boats made of coloured silks; some juggled swords or balls; some walked on ropes or wrestled in contests of strength; some performed magic shows. Presented also were a feature-length song-dance pageant, the "The Prince of Qin Crushing Enemy Battle Formations", and a full-length acrobatic show, "Taiping Music". Emperor Xuan Zong's favourite "Wine-Drinking Music", which featured the spectacular "Dancing Horse", brought the "Grand Celebrations and Feasts" to a climax.

In order to present a false picture of peace and prosperity, the emperor claimed to share happiness with the people and sometimes held grand celebrations and feasts in front of the Flower Tower outside the palace wall. Tens of thousands of commoners came to watch the performances which included magic shows and superb presentations of instrumental music, singing and dancing. Grand celebrations and feasts were also held in the eastern capital Luoyang in front of the Five-Phoenix Building, south of the Tianjin Bridge. The Tang poet Zhang Hu described the scene with the following lines:

His Majesty come east in days of peace,
Grand celebrations and feasts in Luo-
yang city three days in succession.
What superb skill of a boy, balancing on
top of a pole.
Long live the emperor — cheers ring
across the land.

On the day of the grand celebrations and feasts, local officials from various prefectures within the vicinity of 150 kilometres would select the best presentations from their own area to be performed. A large troupe would have as many as several hundred performers who were outstanding in their looks and attractive in their costumes. Even their vehicles were draped in silks and satins and the oxen pulling the vehicles wore masks of fierce beasts or tiger skins. Artists and young apprentices of the Royal Theatre and the "Pear Orchard" were all eager to demonstrate their skills. These celebrations and feasts gradually developed to the point that they resembled a contest of theatrical skills. This promoted the development of acrobatics and many fine items of a special style appeared.

— 42 —

"Only Acrobatic Skills on a Tall Pole
Are So Marvellously Superb"

*The "Hundred Entertainments" in front
of the tower vye with one another in
novelty,
Only acrobatic skills on a tall pole are so
marvelously superb.
Who says the somersaults of the performer in silk gauze are too vigourous?
The supporting acrobat still wishes for
more performers on top.*

The above is an impromptu poem written
by Liu Yan, a 10-year-old child prodigy at the
height of the Tang Dynasty when he watched
acrobat Auntie Wang's performance of balancing a pole on her head at the celebrations and feasts.

The performance of Auntie Wang, an
acrobat famous in "Pole Balancing" from the
Royal Theatre, had an original approach. A
finely carved small wooden hill symbolizing
a legendary fairyland was placed on the tip of
a long pole balanced on her head. A performer, with a sectional whip in his hand, climbed up the pole and displayed all sorts of acrobatic skills amidst the peaks and in the
space between the caves on the wooden hill.
To the accompaniment of the beating of
drums Auntie Wang danced around the
arena. The spectators appreciated the performer's fairylike dancing postures and were
astonished at the strong-woman's effortless
feats. It was no wonder that the child prodigy poet sang of her superb skills. *Jiao
Fang Ji* (*Records of the Royal Theatre*) written
by Cui Lingqin during the Tang Dynasty,
recounts that Emperor Xuan Zong, watching
a performer's execution of handstands and
somersaults on top of a tall pole, could not
help applanding in admiration, saying:

"What marvellous perfection"! and "What
a convincing artistic execution!"

Feats of pole balancing have a long historical tradition in China (Figure 38), and were
prevalent and had attained high levels of
performance before the Tang Dynasty. The
skill only became an integrated, mature artistic masterpiece during the Tang Dynasty.
At that time there were many talented artists
and superb performers. There were not only
court masters of "Pole Balancing" such as
Auntie Wang and Zhao Jiechou but also
many well-known folk acrobats. Each had
his or her unique skills. Some could jump up
and down and dance on the tip of a pole;
some could do accurate acrobatic movements
and some could excel in balancing a pole on
their head with several other performers doing feats at its top. For instance, Shi Huohu,
an acrobat of a minority nationality, developed a style of her own. She put five stiff
bows at the top of a tall pole. Five little girls
climbed up the pole, each stood on the string
of a bow with a weapon in her hands and
performed the full-length song-dance
pageant "The Prince of Qin Crushing Enemy
Battle Formations".

This song and dance pageant consisted of a
dance of acrobatic skills with brave, vigorous
movements in praise of the illustrious military
exploits of Emperor Tai Zong of the Tang
Dynasty, who had the title of the Prince of
Qin before ascending the throne. When
these movements were done at the top of a
pole, the difficulty of acrobatics and the load
suported by the performer playing the base
were enhanced.

It was extraordinarily difficult for a female

38.   Rubbing of a picture of "Pole Balancing" carved on stone in a
Han Dynasty tomb in Anqiu, Shandong Province, and copy of a detail.

performer to act as the base. Just as Wang Jian, a Tang Dynasty poet, described:

> *A pole so heavy that a hundred men can*
> *hardly lift it up,*
> *Rising into blue clouds in mid-air;*
> *A woman with slender waist balances it*
> *with effortless grace,*
> *Lifts it on her head while dancing*
> *to the rhythm of a whole melody.*

"The Queen of Song Touring with Her Entourage", a mural painting in one of the Dunhuang grottoes, depicts the scene more vividly. What is shown in the picture is an acrobat balancing a pole on her head as she walks in front of a long procession. Wearing a short skirt and with a silk sash on her waist, she maintains a graceful dancing posture in the course of advance while displaying superb skills of balance. The beautiful stance of the performer on top of the pole merges into an artistic whole with the dancers in gorgeous costumes on the ground. This is a picture of profound skill and rhythmic beauty (Colour plate 2).

Both the written records and the mural painting reflect the development of the skill of "Pole Balancing" during the Tang Dynasty. There were quite a number of famous female performers of this acrobatic technique. These ancient Chinese women were healthy and strong and presented an image of composure and courage. The performer on top of the pole, usually a woman, displayed gymnastic proficiency and a calm state of mind. This added a tone of lithe and gentle beauty to "Pole Balancing", and strength and beauty to Chinese acrobatics.

Innovations in Rope-Walking Feats

During the Han Dynasty there were already written records of walking on tight ropes. But during the Tang Dynasty new developments were made in rope walking, both in skill and artistry.

Rope walking during the Tang Dynasty was performed mostly around the Qingming Festival, which falls on April 5th or 6th according to the solar calendar. It was a grand performance with the accompaniment of a 100-piece orchestra. Most rope dancers were women who were dressed up in thin silks and gauzes, looking beautiful and dignified. Their high coiffures were fully adorned with pearl and jade ornaments and their feather-like, graceful carriage attracted a large number of admirers. At the beginning of a performance a female acrobat would ascend from the ground, up a slanting rope, to another hori-zontal rope. She would bend from the waist backward and forward, advance and retreat, dance and turn somersaults. These acrobats developed the skill of rope-skipping and sitting down and bouncing up with elasticity. A more breathtaking feat was that of two acrobats exchanging their positions while fencing on the tight rope. This performance was more advanced than those performed during the Han and Jin dynasties when "two artists danced a duet on a rope with shoulders rubbing against each other but remaining firm without tumbling down".

Another special feature of rope walking during the Tang Dynasty was walking in wooden sandals or on stilts on a rope, or forming a human pagoda on a rope suspended high in the air. A series of paintings of "Shinzei's Ancient Music" portray the music, dance and the "Hundred Entertainments" which were introduced from the Tang Dynasty into Japan. This 800-year-old scroll painting, also called "Pictures of Tang Dances", is still preserved in Japan. One picture named "Fairy Ladies Juggling Balls on a Rope" (Figure 39) depicts especially the skills of rope walking. In the picture, all three female performers on the rope wear high-heeled wooden sandals. Two of them are at each end of the rope. One holds a torch in her hand while the other juggles balls. The performer in the centre of the rope also juggles balls. This resembles the modern acrobatic performance of "Feats on a Wire".

39. "Fairy Ladies Juggling Balls on a Rope" in the "Pictures of Tang Dances", a collection of classical Japanese paintings.

Polo Games Depicted in the "Scroll Painting of the Alliance at Bianqiao Bridge"

When Emperor Tai Zong of the Tang Dynasty formed an alliance with a Turkic Khan at Bianqiao Bridge outside Chang'an city in A. D. 626, the Turkic cavalrymen performed an outstanding circus show. Chen Jizhi, a painter of the Song Dynasty (960- 1279), executed a scroll painting based on this historic episode. The painting vividly portrays the superb horsemanship of the minority people during the early Tang Dynasty (Figure 40).

The picture shows 18 men and women

riders in a long procession demonstrating diverse movements of horsemanship. On the left are polo players, a man and a woman, each standing on the back of a galloping horse and chasing after small balls. Musicians are shown playing their instruments while standing on galloping horses, creating a lively atmosphere. Two graceful female riders with coloured kerchiefs in their hands are shown dancing on horseback ahead of the procession of musicians. Outside the arched gate of flags, the painting shows one man doing a handstand on the saddle of a horse, his feet in the air treading on a horizontal staff on which another acrobat performs a handstand. It portrays the unusual performance of double handstands on galloping horseback. Chen Jizhi, painter of the scroll, was well acquainted with the life of the cavalry and so his portrayal is vivid and reliable.

Tang emperors were fond of horsemanship and Emperor Tai Zong (A. D. 599-649) loved to display horsemanship. He taught his generals and warriors martial arts and the art of riding. Emperor Xuan Zong (A.D. 712-756) was a past master at playing polo and taming horses. He personally led a six-member polo team to defeat a team of a dozen members of the Tubos. There was horsemanship training in the army, and demonstrations and races were often held. "Horses Leap Through a Hoop of Swords" was one of these acts in which the cavalrymen galloped on horseback and leaped over hurdles, finally going through a hoop thrust with many sharp swords. Today's circus acts such as "A Horse Goes Through a Paper Drum" and "A Horse Goes Through a Fire Loop" are the continuation and development of these ancient performances of horsemanship.

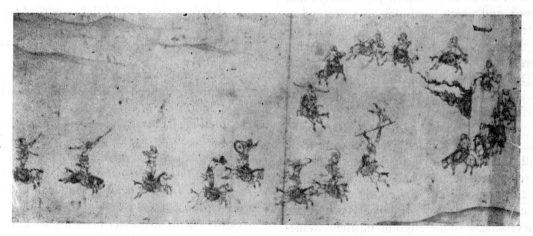

40. Horsemanship — Detail of the Song Dynasty scroll painting "Emperor Tang Tai Zong Makes an Alliance at Bianqiao Bridge".

The "Dancing Horse" at the Height of the Tang Dynasty

The "Dancing Horse" was a show of horsemanship popular at the height of the Tang Dynasty. It differed from the demonstration of skills of men or women riding on horseback in that horses were trained to dance by themselves. The earliest records of dancing horses in ancient historical books describe "the dancing of horses coming from different parts of the country" at the imperial court at the end if the Xia Dynasty (c. 21st century-16th century B.C.). Also recorded are horses pulling the chariots of emperors of the Zhou Dynasty (c. 11th century-256 B.C.) and marching to the rhythm of music. In the period of the Southern and Northern Dynasties, a red horse in Henan region is described which could kneel, pay homage and dance, and which local officials presented as a tribute to the emperor. All of these records attest to the early origin of dancing horses.

During the Kaiyuan and Tianbao reigns (A.D. 713-756), the dancing of horses was performed on a spectacular scale. On the day of grand celebrations and feasts, 100 horses often came out together to demonstrate their skill. During their performance the horses were draped in silks and embroidery, decorated with gold and silver fittings, and their manes were adorned with pearls and jade. They danced to the rhythm of the "Wine-Drinking Music", with their heads high and tails curled. They marched in step, advancing and retreating in close harmony with the music. At the climax a young rider on horseback rode into the arena and leapt up onto a three-decked "lacquered couch". The horse, with the rider on its back, spun around on the towering lacquered couch. Finally, a strongman came into the arena, and with both hands, lifted up the couch on which the horse continued to prance. The famous Tang poet, Du Fu, described this action in a line of poetry "A horse performing posturing dances was skilled at climbing the decks of the couch". After dancing, the horse cleverly knelt and bowed in four directions, then held a wine cup in its mouth to toast the guests. Hence, the act was also called, "Dancing Horse Holds a Wine Cup in its Mouth". Zhang Yue, a Tang poet, in his poem written for music, entitled, "Dancing Horse Proclaims the Emperor's Longevity for a Thousand Autumns", says,

> The emperor's supreme benevolence matches the sky's,
> A fine horse comes for an audience from the Western Regions,
> It canters slowly on its knees to pay respect,
> Unbridled, arrogant, refusing to advance,
> Marking time a thousand steps on the spot,
> Bristling its mane and pawing all the time.
> Raring itself up in a rage, it suddenly leaps onto the high couch.
> More thrilling, it holds a wine cup in its mouth at the end of the feasting and music,
> Bowing its head and drooping its tail, it appears to be dead drunk.

This poem conveys the lively emotions and the spectacular performance of the dancing horse. The horse is described as urging the guests to drink to their hearts' content, thus enhancing the gaiety of the atmosphere. "Dancing Horse" was an act greatly enjoyed at the height of the Tang Dynasty.

Records of dancing horses were verified by

imagery on a silver ewer from the Tang Dynasty unearthed in 1970 in Hejia Village on Xi'an's southern outskirts. (Colour plate 3). Gilded in relief on the exquisite ewer is a horse with a plump body and with its hind legs squatting. It holds a wine cup in its mouth while remaining in a kneeling posture, paying homage. Its tail is waving and its mane tied with long ribbons of silk gauze, which appear to be fluttering in the wind. The horse seems to be urging guests to drink.

New Developments in Animal Taming

During the Tang Dynasty, apart from highly developed horsemanship, other tamed animal performances also made rapid progress. Acrobats demonstrated their diverse skills, ranging from taming rhinoceroses and elephants to coaching insects and ants. From the material recorded in Zheng Xi's rhyme-prose, "Watching a Hundred Animals Dance at Hanyuan Hall on Lunar New Year's Day", it is learned that rhinoceroses and elephants were able to spin around, dance, kneel and pay homage. Even hedgehogs could ring bells and small creatures such as house lizards could dance, arranging themselves in a procession.

Monkey shows were the most developed in the category of tamed animal performances during the middle and late Tang Dynasty. Rich in content, they spread over vast areas. People even brought skilled monkeys to celebrations for successful candidates of the imperial civil examination and to assemblies for paying homage to the emperor. Some persons were even appointed as officials because they were proficient in the art of monkey taming. Monkeys were able to climb up poles, do somersaults and hold races on dog back, as well as to imitate many human movements. They were much loved by audiences, being clever, humourous and arousing laughter.

"Cock-Fighting" is an animal show as famous as the dancing horse and the tamed monkey. The court established an "Imperial cock-training farm" where more than 1,000 cocks of excellent breed were collected and cared for. Cock raising was also popular among the common people. At the time of Emperor Xuan Zong of the Tang Dynasty there was a young cock-trainer named Jia Chang. It was said that the cocks under his direction could stand in a row on a square and advance and retreat in formation, varying their steps with the motion of the whip. When the winner or loser of a contest had been decided upon, the stronger would march in front and the weaker behind, moving in formation like wild geese in the sky.

From these records it is learned that as early as 1,500 years ago in China there were many animal shows, both short and long, in which animals displayed superb skills. Many circus acts today have developed from these early animal shows.

"Taiping Music" and "Lion Dance"

An animal masquerade, called the "Lion Dance", has already been mentioned in written records of the Wei, Jin and the Southern and Northern Dynasties. But at that time the movements of the dance were rather simple. The dance was often used as a prelude to a larger programme at a temple fair. But the "Lion Dance" during the Tang Dynasty was quite different. In particular, the "Taiping Music" at the height of the Tang Dynasty, also called "Five Different Lions", was very spectacular (Figure 41). According to records in *Jiu Tang Shu* (*Old History of the Tang Dynasty*), written by Liu Xu and others of the Later Jin Dynasty (A. D. 936-946), "Five Different Lions" was a featurelength presentation, performed in an open square. Five masqueraded lions, each more than three metres tall, wearing pelts of five different colours would be teased by 12 performers who were called lion boys. Each lion boy was dressed up as a boy of the Western Regions and carried a red horsetail whisk in his hand. Teased by them, the lions would bend forward and backward in a lively manner. The performance was accompanied by the beating of drums and sprightly rhythms of Kucina music. A 140-member chorus sang the "Taiping Music". The atmosphere was both solemn and lively during this presentation of the "Lion Dance" at the imperial court.

During the Tang Dynasty the "Lion Dance" was also very popular among the common people. It was presented for the army and at temple fairs. Bai Juyi, a famous Tang Dynasty poet, in a lyric poem entitled "Dance of the Western Regions", passionately described a performance of the "Lion Dance", as follows:

> *Dance of the Western Regions, performers masquerade as a lion and men of the northern Hu tribe.*

41. "Lion Dance" in the Japanese "Pictures of Tang Dances".

The lion's head is carved of wood and the
tail made of silk,
Gilt eyes and silver teeth.
Bristling mane and ears perked up.
They have come as if from shifting sands
over three thousand miles,
The two men of the northern Hu tribe,
With purple whiskers and deep-set eyes.
Rejoicing and prancing, they come for-
ward to say,
"It was prior to the fall of Liangzhou,
When Viceroy of Anxi came in."
A short while later there comes more
news,
"The way leading to Anxi has been cut
off and now it is impossible to return
there."
Facing the lion, with tears streaming
down,
"Have you known the fall of Liangzhou?"

The lion turns its head around, gazing
westward, Roaring plaintively, causing
the spectators to grieve in sympathy! ...

In this poem Bai Juyi recounts that the masquerade lion was made of silk, with golden eyes and silver teeth, and that its appearance was majestic. Moreover, he indicates that it demonstrated acrobatic skills, shaking its head and wagging its ears in high spirits, while teased by performers who were dressed up as lion boys of minority nationalities with brown whiskers and deep-set eyes. And, through the fine performance of the lion and the lion boys, he depicts the lion's homesick sentiments to inspire the militant fervour of generals and warriors in frontier areas for recovering the lost land (Colour plates 4 and 5).

"Sword Dance" and "Swinging Meteors"

The "Sword Dance" was a new act first mentioned in written records of the Tang Dynasty. There have been different descriptions of this dance, some describing it as a woman performer in martial attire dancing with a sword (some say, with a luminous object) in her hand. Others describe her as dancing with a silk ribbon with two luminous objects, one at each end of the ribbon. Judging from "On Seeing a Pupil of Lady Gongsun Perform the Sword Dance", a poem written by Du Fu, a famous Tang Dynasty poet, the art of the "Sword Dance" is identical with "Swinging Meteors" as performed in modern acrobatics. In Qing times, the people in Gansu Province and other outlying regions called "meteors" "sword-like objects".

In A.D. 767, Du Fu watched a sword dance performed by a woman, Li the Twelfth, at the home of a friend in Sichuan. He learned that she had been taught by Lady Gongsun and he could not help recalling his childhood, 50 years prior, when he had watched a "Sword Dance" performed with strength and freedom by Lady Gongsun. He wrote a poem to convey his thoughts.

There was once a lovely woman, Lady
Gongsun,
Whose performance of the "Sword
Dance" amazed the whole world.
Onlookers watched her, feeling dizzy sen-
sations
As she made heaven and earth appear
to plunge and soar.

Her sword flashed and it was like the nine
falling suns shot by Yi the archer.
She leapt and you thought a crowd of
gods bestrode a soaring dragon!
She advanced like a peal of thunder, with
the rage of a gathering storm;
She ceased like rivers and seas frozen
with glittering ice.

Resorting to natural scenery and ancient mythological tales, the poet vividly described the rapidly swinging meteors with profound artistry and a romantic touch.

"Swinging Meteors" has been evolved from the meteor rope. As early as in primitive society, there emerged a method of hunting wild animals by tying sharp stones to a rope. This implement was called a meteor rope. Later, the stones at the two ends of the rope were replaced by coloured balls, bowls filled with water, or fire balls. Various patterns of spinning and whirling were formed and came to be described as "waves rolling and foaming", "meteors chasing the moon" and "butterflies flying". Artistic handling enhanced the appeal and it became one of the favourite acrobatic acts viewed by the people. Well-known artists Lady Gongsun and Lady Li the Twelfth of the Royal Theatre were past masters at "Swinging Meteors". They produced far-reaching effects both at the imperial court and among the people. It was said that Zhang Xu and Huai Su, renowned Tang calligraphers, improved vastly in their cursive hand, showing both strength and rhythm, after watching Lady Gongsun's performance. After attending her exquisite performances, women also imitated the style of Lady Gongsun's costume.

New Developments in Magic

Tang Dynasty magic both inherited traditional skills handed down from the Han Dynasty and introduced many new tricks from abroad. An endless stream of new items emerged. The best of these was "Entering Jar Dance" introduced from the Korean Peninsula. This was performed by having a flattened round jar placed on each of two square low tables. A performer would enter the mouth of the jar on the right, both feet extending upward, his whole body vanishing into the jar. At the same time another person would come out of the jar on the left, lifting his arms high (Figure 42). This act has been handed down and is called, "Disappearing in a Jar" today. Another form of disappearing act was "Entering Horse Belly Dance", that is, a man vanishing into the belly of a horse. This was also first mentioned in the records of that time (Figure 43).

"Lying on Sword Dance" was a magic show introduced from India. Brahmins presented it during the reign of Emperor Rui Zong (A. D. 710-712). Lying on the tip of a sharp knife, a performer could play a musical instrument.

He remained unscathed after finishing a melody. It may be said that this type of performance introduced torture tricks into Chinese magic, and it was the earliest record of such magic (Figure 44).

Emperors of the Tang Dynasty worshipped Taoism and esteemed Taoist priests. Therefore, a number of magicians appeared in the guise of immortals to win the favour of emperors and influential officials. There

42. "Entering Jar Dance" in the Japanese "Pictures of Tang Dances".

imperial examination. His supernatural powers were described as follows:

> Travelling over the North Sea in the
>   morning,
> And visiting Guangxi, south China in the
>   evening,
> Audacious, with a blue snake in his
>   sleeves.
> He has come thrice to Yueyang incognito,
> Reciting aloud while flying across the
>   Dongting Lake.

have been spread many stories about the Eight Immortals. Lü Dongbin, one of the Eight Immortals, whom modern folk magicians honoured as the founder of their craft was, in fact, a scholar who failed to pass the imperial examination.

The magic art of Han Xiangzi, another of the Eight Immortals, was to instantly brew wine in a small gourd and plant lotus in a flaming jar and make it blossom. Taoist priest Ye Fashan's method of transferring people or objects from one place to another was even more miraculous. It is said that he led Emperor Xuan Zong of the Tang Dynasty to the palace on the moon where the emperor copied down the "Song of Rainbow-Coloured Feathered Costumes", his favourite tune. Most of the supernatural art of Taoist priests was achieved through performing magic tricks, and the marvellous

43. "Entering Horse Belly Dance" in the Japanese "Pictures of Tang Dances".

— 53 —

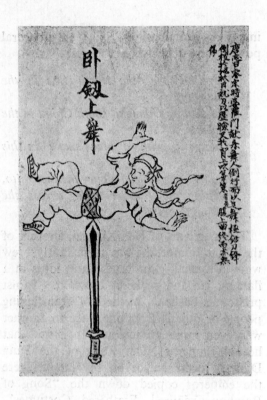

卧劍上舞

legends about these priests have provided materials for magic shows in subsequent dynasties. "Taking Wine from an Empty Wine Pot" and "Flowers Appearing Out of a Brazier", are two examples of this.

44. "Lying on Sword Dance" in the Japanese "Pictures of Tang Dances".

The Rising Art of the "Human Pagoda"

Prior to the Tang Dynasty, the "Human Pagoda" was seldom seen. This artistic performance from the Tang Dynasty can be found in both written records and pictures. It even spread abroad and has been preserved in the acrobatic skills of other countries.

Shi Huohu, previously mentioned as a skilful performer of "Pole Balancing" during the Tang Dynasty, was also skilled in the art of performing the "Human Pagoda". These skills were displayed standing on top of small tables piled up in five tiers. This extremely strong female acrobat had performers standing on her shoulders four tiers high. When she gave the signal, the performers extended their hands at the same time, looking like a pagoda towering into the blue sky. It was a thrilling

spectacle.

A picture of the "Human Pagoda" painted on a bow (Figure 45) preserved from the Tang Dynasty provides an image of this art. The acrobat who forms the base is shown in a horse-riding stance, bending both knees equally. He carries two performers on his shoulders and on their shoulders stands the third person on top of whom stands the fourth person with both hands lifted up. The five performers together form a four-tiered human pagoda.

The art of performing the "Human Pagoda" requires physical prowess and coordination in the movements of the waist and legs, as well as skill in performing the handstand. Moreover, it requires all persons

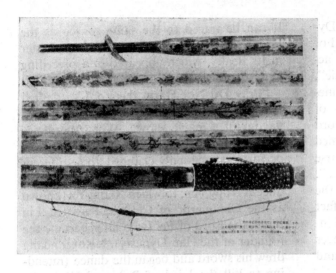

45. Painted bow from the Tang Dynasty stored in the Japanese Shoso-in Museum, and copy of a detail of the picture on the painted bow.

taking part in the performance to have good balance and grace. The emergence of this art illustrates that Tang Dynasty acrobatics paid great attention to the training of the human body. Presenting group performances and showing a great variety of skills in one act enriched the artistic image of acrobatics of that time.

Since the Tang Dynasty, the "Human Pagoda" has become a major act in acrobatic performances. Today's "Gigantic Pyramid", "Lesser Pyramid" and "Group Cycling" have been developed from this act.

Acrobatics in Music and Dance

Music, dance and acrobatics came from one source and were closely interrelated through out history and particularly during the Tang Dynasty. Artists often accompanied or interspersed music and dance with acrobatics.

Many acrobatic items during the Tang Dynasty were called "dance" or "music". For instance, the "Lion Dance", a genuine acrobatic item, was called "Taiping Music", and the "Dancing Horse" was called "Wine-Drinking Music". The performance of "Swinging Meteors" was called the "Sword Dance". Even magic shows were named "Entering Jar Dance", "Entering Horse Belly Dance" and "Lying on Sword Dance", and treading on wooden balls was called the "Whirling Dance of Hu Tribes". The fact that "dance" and "music", were included in their titles implies that these performances were presented by combining dance and music with gymnastic skills.

Many dances worthy of the name also contained acrobatic skills. For instance, "the Prince of Qin Crushing Enemy Battle Formations" at the time of Emperor Tai Zong of the Tang Dynasty was a vigorous dance with weapons. This performance was related to the competitive contests with five types of weapons which was already popular during the time of the Southern and Northern Dynasties.

The full length music and dance performance, "Bird Greets Longevity of the Empress" at the time of Empress Wu Zetian (A.D. 624-705) was a bird masquerade.

It can be traced to the same source as the bird masquerade "Phoenix Holds a Letter in Its Beak", which appeared in a preceding dynasty.

"Pray Do Not Harm the Lord", adapted from an historical episode, had the rich flavour of a magic show. When the dance reached its climax, all the costumes of the performers suddenly changed to a different hue. The episode described how at the banquet at Hongmen, to which Xiang Yu (known as the Conqueror of Chu) had invited Liu Bang, the Lord of Pei (who later became the founder of the Han Dynasty), Xiang Zhuang drew his sword and began the dance (intending to kill the Lord of Pei), and Xiang Bo followed suit, shielding Liu Bang with his body so that Xiang Zhuang could not strike him.

"Bayu Drum Dance" and "Bodhidharma Entertainment" used many skills of martial arts, and some performers were acrobats as well as dancing stars, such as the acrobat Lady Gongsun. The use and intermingling of music and dance with acrobatics, as well as the introduction of the "Comic Dialogue Show" and the "Puppet Show", promoted the development of the performing arts during the Tang Dynasty.

Acrobatic Exchange Between China and Other Countries

During the reign of Tai Zong of the Tang Dynasty, diplomatic activities were extensive. According to statistics from the early Tang Dynasty, more than 10,000 households in Luoyang were envoys, students and merchants from Southeast Asia, the Western Regions, Central Asia, and even Persia and the Roman Empire. The emperor pursued an open-door policy, assimilating into the culture diverse forms of music, dance and entertainment. This policy promoted cultural exchange among the different nationalities of China, and between China and other countries.

Of all the music and dances at the height of the Tang Dynasty, half came from China's minority nationalities or from abroad. "Tri-Stick Drum" (a kind of Indian drum played with three sticks by a musician with a third stick always suspended in mid-air) and "Ascetic Practices" of India, as well as "Ball Games" of Southeast Asia and "Magic Shows" of Korea, are examples of performances introduced from abroad. The "Whirling Dance" from Central Asia was especially popular.

The "Whirling Dance" was performed in the following fashion: An artist trod on a wooden ball two-thirds of a metre in diameter, performing a dance of whirling around like a cyclone on the surface of the rolling ball. The dancer would advance, retreat and spin, but never let her feet leave the ball. When she trod on the ball, it made the sound of "rat-ta-ta-ta." Hence it was called "Rat-ta-ta-ta Dance". A Tang poet described this dance in the following lines:

> Like a precious pearl found under the
>   Black Dragon's chin,
> The ball advances and retreats, vanishing
>   as fast as a shooting star in the sky.
> A maiden with flushed cheeks, waving a
>   light scarf,
> Spins around just like lightning.

At the height of the Tang Dynasty, there were a large number of performers of the "Whirling Dance" in the Royal Theatre. Several hundred pretty women in court costumes often demonstrated their skills. Standing on wooden balls in formation, they moved to and fro, forward and backward, treading with effortless ease. They sometimes changed the patterns of their formation. Sometimes they lifted their arms and wave their hands; sometimes they twisted and whirled around. When several hundred wooden balls were rolling, it sounded like the rumbling of thunder and made a spectacular scene. At that time people, ranging from ladies-in-waiting at the court to commoners, loved this game and many were good at treading on such balls. Both Yang Yuhuan, the favourite concubine of Emperor Xuan Zong, and An Lushan, ringleader of the An-Shi Rebellion, excelled in this game.

While assimilating foreign music, dance and entertainment, the culture of China also spread in all directions. Chinese culture produced a fairly deep-going impact on Japan, its neighbour in the East, and quite a number of pieces of music, dance and acrobatics have been handed down to the present. Spread to Japan were, for example, "Dancing in the Flames of Fire", "Melon Growing", "Tree Planting", and "Vanishing Acts" in the category of magic shows. Also spread were feats of physical prowess such as the "Human Pyramid" and the "Lion Dance". The Japanese have called these "Monkey Feats", or more explicitly "Foreign Feats", to explain that they came from abroad.

A number of cultural relics, now still preserved in Japan, are excellent evidences of the long-term exchange of acrobatics between China and Japan. For instance, a Tang Dynasty bow is stored in Shoso-in, the large storehouse northwest of the Buddhist hall in Todaiji, a temple in Nara. It was one of the rare objects which the royal house of Japan donated to Todaiji in the first year of the Zhide reign of Emperor Su Zong (A. D. 756) in the Tang Dynasty. Grand acrobatic performances were painted all over the back of the bow. The picture included two sets of "Pole Balancing" performances (Figure 46) and two sets of "Human Pyramid" performances.

"Pictures of Tang Dances", called "Shinzei's Ancient Music", are pictures of Tang Dynasty music performances, dancing and the "Hundred Entertainments", which Japanese artists time and again hand-copied and handed down. Depicted in them are a number of acrobatic acts including "Swallowing a Knife", "Spitting Fire", "Juggling Balls", "Rope Walking", "Handstands on Shoulders", "Four-Performer Pyramid", "Entering Jar Dance" and "Lion Dance". These acts not only spread to Japan, but have also been handed down and developed in China (Figures 47, 48, 49, 50, 51, 52 & 53).

46. "Pole Balancing" — Two copies of details of the picture on the painted bow from the Tang Dynasty.

47. "Four-Performer Pyramid" in the "Pictures of Tang Dances".

— 58 —

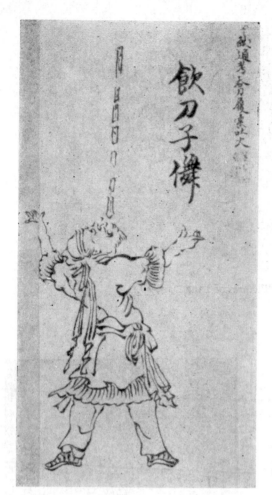

50. "Handstand on shoulders in the "Pictures of Tang Dances".

48. "Swallowing a Knife", a magic act in the "Pictures of Tang Dances".

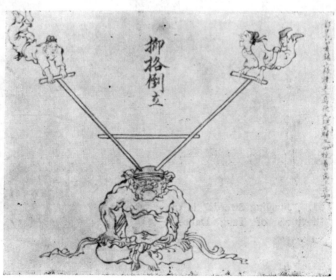

49. "Duet Handstands on Poles Balanced on a Third Performer's Head" in the "Pictures of Tang Dances".

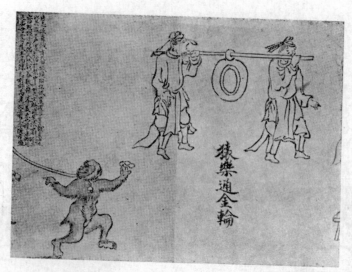

52. "Tamed Monkey" in the "Pictures of Tang Dances".

51. "Juggling Swords" in the "Pictures of Tang Dances".

53. Spitting Fire" in the "Pictures of Tang Dances".

— 60 —

5. Back to the Commoners *(A.D. 960-1368)*

China once again fell into a state of disintegration and confusion after the collapse of the Tang Dynasty. The period became known in history as the Five Dynasties and Ten States (A. D. 907-979). In A. D. 960 Zhao Kuangyin founded the Song Dynasty, then unified the whole country and set up its capital in Bianliang (present-day Kaifeng, Henan). Under the unified state power, feudal economy, culture and art made rapid progress. In A. D. 1127, the Kingdom of Kin founded by the Nuzhens in the north, seized the capital Bianliang. Zhao Gou, Prince of Kang and son of Emperor Hui Zong (A.D. 1082-1135), went south and crossed the Yangtze and the Huai rivers. Known as Emperor Gao Zong of the Song Dynasty, he established the capital at Lin'an (present-day Hangzhou) and this new regime is historically known as the Southern Song Dynasty. It was later destroyed by the Yuan Dynasty (A. D. 1271-1368), founded by the Mongols.

Reviewing Chinese history, we realize that the Song Dynasty was the period when feudal society was fairly well developed. Compared with the preceding Sui-Tang period, the small-scale peasant economy of the Song Dynasty was more prosperous and feudal cities thrived. Consequently, townspeople introduced new features in to Song Dynasty culture and art. In literature, it was the emergence and development of the storytellers' scripts; in art, it was the gradual division among different types of performing arts such as, music, dance, drama, comic shows and puppet shows. Only acrobatics survived from what had been commonly grouped together under the Tang Dynasty as music and the "Hundred Entertainments". What was known as the "Hundred Entertainments" during the Song Dynasty included only acrobatics. Since acrobatic art had a long-standing history, it was still predominant among the many categories of performing arts.

During the Song Dynasty changes took place in the organization of acrobatic troupes. They were roughly divided into two categories, government-run and private-owned. Government-run troupes included the Left and Right Troops that performed the "Hundred Entertainments" in the army. The private-owned troupes which gave performances for which they charged money, presented shows in curtained-off arenas or on makeshift stages encircled by carved balustrades (abbreviated as "balustrade stage"). Strolling performers gave shows in the streets or in other public places. Some performances were sponsored by the government for the celebration of an emperor's birthday, carrying on the old tradition of the Sui-Tang period. Others were jointly sponsored by the government and the people, such as entertainments for the Lantern Festival or at temple fairs. According to rough estimates, the Song Dynasty had more than 120 acrobatic numbers and the skills showed novelty, cleverness and proficiency, exceeding the performances of former times.

Since the acrobats of the Song Dynasty had close ties with the townspeople, peasants and other labouring people, their skills were brimming with the flavour of life. And since acrobatic art had left the palaces and halls of the feudal ruling class and was close to the people, it was despised by the feudal landlord class and was discriminated against. Especially, during the late Southern Song Dynasty when the rational philosophy or neo-Confucianism of Cheng Yi (A. D. 1033-1107) and

Zhu Xi (A. D. 1130-1200) occupied a dominant position, it was considered unrefined. Later the ruling class, during the Yuan Dynasty (A. D. 1271-1368), took over the prejudices of the feudal scholars of the Song Dynasty so the status of acrobatic art and acrobats continued to decline. Nevertheless, acrobatics was still lively and developed among the people. It continued to fascinate the commoners and a number of intellectuals. For many years artists dedicated themselves to acrobatic art and made it possible to hand this art down from generation to generation.

The "Hundred Entertainments" in the Army

The capitals of the Song Dynasty established the acrobatic troupes of the Left and Right Troops. Bianjing, the capital of Northern Song, and Lin'an, the capital of Southern Song, often held grand theatrical performances, with the performers of the Left and Right Troops as the main body with assistance from folk artists.

Dong Jing Meng Hua Lu (*Memories of the Eastern Capital*), written by Meng Yuanlao of the Southern Song Dynasty, records the army's "Hundred Entertainments" which Zhao Jie, Emperor Hui Zong, watched in front of Baojin Tower in Kaifeng in the late years of the Northern Song Dynasty. The description from these records is as follows:

Curtains were put up and flags hoisted all over the open square in front of the tower, and at the entrance and exit. At the beginning of the performance, a musician, holding a rattle-drum in his hand and escorted by a dozen other drummers, addressed the audience. Then, with lively musical accompaniment, a strongman with a red turban around his head waved a huge flag and performers, masquerading as lions, tigers and leopards,

came in prancing and rollicking. Thus started the prelude to a grand acrobatic performance. Then a performer brandished two flags and many acrobats skilled in martial arts performed somersaults in coordination with the flag brandishing. Meanwhile, performances of "Pole Climbing" and "Pole Balancing" were put on in the midst of the crowd.

After doing somersaults to the melodious rhythms of the lute, more than 100 warriors in short, close-fitting attire came into the arena, with long pheasant feathers in one hand and a shield or wooden knife or spear in the other and performed duets of acrobatic fighting.

At the firing of guns, the martial arts acrobats withdrew. A display of fireworks then spurted out from all sides and "gods and spirits" appeared in the midst of fiery trees and silvery flowers. It was a unique magic show. Performers with masks on their heads, spat mists and brandished knives and swords.

After the "gods and spirits" had disappeared, about 100 warriors performed group fighting. They combined wrestling with various other techniques, such as throwing knives on the ground, then doing somersaults and picking up the knives from the ground. When all the spectators were in a high state of tension, comic actors came onto the arena. They were dressed up as countryfolk and presented a scene depicting an argument between a husband and wife. The peasant then made his exit, carrying his wife on his back, thus arousing hilarious laughter among the spectators. After the brief comic act, famous artists of that time put on some excellent performances, followed by a fascinating circus show.

The riders came onto the arena one by one, posing in different stances, brandishing heavy halberds and lifting stone locks. Then, more than 100 women horseback riders galloped to the facade of the tower. Clad in multi-coloured, embroidered war robes and with their horses adorned with gold and jade fittings, they combined the appearance of vigour and charm. They galloped around the arena on fine steeds, changing formation, fighting each other and turning backward to shoot arrows. They then all came to the front of the tower and got off their horses to pay homage to the court, and quickly leapt up onto their horses and galloped away. It was a show full of variety.

Finally, there were the polo matches of the male riders, with their contests of skill. At that time polo games were played either on donkey back or horseback. The games on horseback were more fierce, involving a greater number of players. They brought the entire programme to a climax.

This joint performance consisted mainly of acrobatic acts such as martial arts, magic, variety and circus shows and comic acts. It is evident that the Song Dynasty encouraged the acrobatic arts, carrying on the tradition of the Sui-Tang period. During the early Song Dynasty the country was in the initial stage of its establishment and the trend of setting great store by martial skills was still prevalent. The performances were bold and vigorous, and soldiers acted as performers. But the comic act "Husband and Wife Grapple with Each Other" showed that townspeople's literature and art influenced acrobatic performances. In short, the Northern Song Dynasty was a transitional period in the style of acrobatic art.

The Festival of the Imperial Birthday

The emperors of the Song Dynasty paid great attention to their birthdays, naming them the "Festival of the Imperial Birthday". Grand celebrations were held every year. Sumptuous banquets were held and theatrical performances, many of them acrobatics, were presented during the feasting (Colour plate 6).

The programme usually began with vocal mimicry, such as "A Hundred Birds Chirp", followed by toasting. A dozen and sometimes more than 20 toasts would be drunk at a banquet, and theatrical performances would be presented in between the toasts. During the Northern Song Dynasty, group acrobatic performances were usually given on the occasion of the third toast. Many diverse items were presented on the stage at the same time, including "Gymnastics on Pole", "Rope Twirling", "Handstands", "Callisthenics", "Snake Tricks", "Pyramid of Bowls", "Kicking Vases", "Turning Somersaults" and "Human Pyramid". These would be the most spectacular presentations throughout the feasting. There were also shows on the occasions of other toasts, but smaller in scale. Most of them were vocal solos and instrumental music, dancing puppets, brief song and dance acts, and acrobatics and magic shows. All were symbolic of a birthday celebration. For instance, among the magic shows performed by magician Yao Run was "Setting Free the Captive Bird", in which a bird was conjured up from among peaches offered as a birthday present.

Another of his acts was a performer lifting a child masquerading as the God of Longevity.

More than 170 performers took part in the programme of the Festival of the Imperial Birthday, and among them were 115 acrobats. Most acrobats were folk artists who were summoned to perform for this special occasion, which reflected the decline of court acrobatics and the rise of folk acrobatics.

The Rise of the "Curtained-Off Arena" and the "Balustrade Stage"

The curtained-off arenas which arose during the time of the Song Dynasty represented the primary form of popular pleasure houses. In a demarcated area of a flourishing city, a plot of ground would be draped all around with curtains and spectators would gather there to watch performances. Such a place was called a "curtained-off arena". For the convenience of performance, carved balustrades were put up inside the arena to partition off a makeshift stage. A curtained-off arena would contain two or several "balustrade stages". The largest "curtained-off arena" in the Bianjing capital had 13 "balustrade stages" where different kinds of entertainment could be put on at the same time. During the Southern Song Dynasty, Lin'an city had 23 "curtained-off arenas". At that time the downtown section of Lin'an city near Zhong'an Bridge had a continuous stream of spectators and was a scene of much activity.

The "curtained-off arenas" and the "balustrade stages" were spots for the performances of professional artists. They vyed with one another to earn a livelihood, each presenting something unusual to try to beat their rivals. Thus they propelled forward the development of the "Hundred Entertainments" so

that at that time there were many artists famed for their superb skills. For instance, Ren Xiaosan's "Stick Puppets", Zhang Miaozhen's "Rope Walking", Bao Xi's "Magic" and Jin Shihao's "Water Puppets" were considered fascinating. In "curtained-off arenas" feats of physical prowess and wrestling were most popular. There were not only many famous male wrestling experts but also quite a number of strong women wrestlers. Their movements combined firmness, vigour and agility. In addition to the performance of acrobatic acts the "curtained-off arenas" also provided sheds for "lantern riddles" and sports games and spots for displaying flowers, rare birds and animals. The "balustrade stages" could shelter the spectators from wind and rain and provided a place to present shadow shows. During the Song Dynasty there were already facilities for lighting as well as shielding the light. The performances attracted a large crowd of spectators and brought together and trained many performers.

Nevertheless, the performers had only a meagre income. For at that time the "curtained-off arenas" did not sell tickets and the spectators would only donate as much money as they pleased. Sometimes the performers failed to collect any money, so they had no guaranteed livelihood. Regardless of this, only well-known, top-grade performers with superb skills were qualified to perform in "curtained-off arenas" and on "balustrade stages". Performers below that level had no chance to go there; they could only give outdoor shows at a village entrance or on the roadside. These were the "strolling performers", and there were great numbers of them.

Various kinds of folk artists during the Song and Yuan dynasties were known as "strolling performers", especially those performers who gave touring shows. They led a vagrant life, roaming here and there to sell their art. As they performed most of the time in open squares, on public grounds or on street corners, these performances were called "roadside performances", and were considered to be insignificant entertainment and of low status. These "roadside performances" were continued from the time of the Song Dynasty and became a way out for earning a livelihood for most of the acrobats in the old society.

There was another category of acrobats who performed "Village Hundred Entertainments" which came into being during the Song Dynasty. They were poverty-stricken peasants, who roamed the cities to eke out a living by giving performances. They performed impromptu at the call of whomsoever wanted to see the shows. "Strolling performers" and "Village Hundred Entertainments" performers usually gave shows as a family group, men and women, old and young, and so developed the style of making a living through family performances.

Folk acrobatic troupes developed into guilds as performers of the same skills, either because of having been trained under the same master or for vocational ties, grouped together naturally. The smaller ones were called *huo* (group) and the larger ones *she* (commune). These guild organizations united the performers, encouraged the improvement of professional skills and propelled the advance of acrobatics. This played a significant role in bringing about the division of the "Hundred Entertainments" and the branching out of various performing arts as well as the establishment of different schools.

Juggling with the Hands and Feet

More than 120 acrobatic items were performed during the Song Dynasty. And records of that time often used "Juggling with the Hands or Feet" to describe all items of acrobatics, and jugglers with the hands or feet of the "Hundred Entertainments" were called acrobats. This shows the high esteem in which juggling with the hands and feet was held during the Song Dynasty. As a result, these two branches of skill made great progress. "Juggling Balls or Swords" with the hands were already popular in ancient times but developed new achievements during the Song Dynasty. For instance, "Juggling a

Buddhist Staff" (an item performed by monks) and "Juggling Waist-Drum Sticks" (with the third stick always suspended in mid-air, an act reportedly introduced from India) were warmly received by a vast audience.

"Juggling with the Feet" was also developed from the original skills of treading on balls or on stilts. Performers at that time were able to kick a bottle so that it would loop high into the air and land upside down on the tip of a distant staff or onto a ball. Other items such as "Juggling Bowls", "Juggling Bells", "Juggling Chime Stones" and "Juggling Writing Brushes and Inksticks" emerged one after another. In addition, there appeared "Juggling Jars", which was performed while lying down, feet extended upward. This represents the primary form of "Juggling with the Feet" performed in modern times.

A game of football was well-developed during the Song Dynasty, and it was often depicted in works of literature. Some games were held as a contest and others were purely in the nature of an acrobatic display. For instance, "catching the ball with every part of the body" was an acrobatic performance in which a performer used his head, shoulders, back arms, chest, abdomen or knees to kick the ball in place of his feet.

New Horseback Riding Skills

During the Song Dynasty, horsemanship attained a new level, and some patterns devised at that time continue to be essential movements in circus shows at present. The warriors in the Left and Right Troops of the Northern Song Dynasty demonstrated splendid equestrian skills. The equestrian parade began with a warrior riding unarmed into the arena or waving a huge flag while on horseback. The performance focused on archery. A cavalry man would throw a red embroidered silk ball tied with red ribbons to the ground while galloping at full speed. Riders, chasing after him, would attempt to shoot at the ball with bows and arrows, and riders with superb skill could bend their bows with both hands and display different skills. Another archery skill was "Shooting at a Willow Twig". A willow twig was planted on the ground, and riders on galloping horses would shoot at it. Their arrows were equipped with a special type of arrowhead shaped like a tiny crescent-shaped shovel. The willow twig, when hit, was cut off by the shovel. There was great skill involved to be able to hit so small a target while riding on a galloping horse.

Wielding objects while on horseback was another distinctive characteristic of circus performances during the Song Dynasty. Riders would often wield halberds, swords and other heavy objects while on horseback. For instance, they would wield cart wheels with 10 multi-coloured flags hoisted on them. The riders were strong, vigorous and able to display stunts such as standing on horseback, doing handstands, vaulting over a horse, presenting a saddle, suddenly dipping below the horse's belly while their feet were still in the stirrups, chasing another horse and other skills of horsemanship (Figure 54).

In an act called "Leopard Horse", the movements were brave and unrestrained. In this act, a fine steed galloped in advance and a brave warrior caught up with it in big strides, grabbing at the horse's tail and leaping onto the horse's back. This skill has been handed down in China for 1,000 years, and at the national acrobatic festival in 1961 a veteran acrobat of Shandong Province demonstrated this movement, called "Catching a Saddleless Horse in Eight Strides". It thrilled the whole audience.

Magic

Scientific and technological progress provided facilities for the creation of magic shows. New items of magic emerged and specialization developed. For example,

54. Picture of a handstand on a galloping horse's
back on a porcelain pillow from the Song Dynasty.

some magicians specialized in the art of transferring things from one place to another, called "Hiding Tricks". A magician could instantly conjure up large basins and bowls, similar to today's "Traditional-Style Conjuring", and could even conjure up a real man.

There were also brief magic acts called "Sleight of Hand". For example, a magician could conjure up rice from an empty bowl and when he put two bowls together, the rice would be transformed into delicious wine. Chinese magic continues to arouse interest, confounding people with its mystery.

"Sleight of Hand" became a special branch of magic. Its representative work was called "Clay Ball". This type of magic trick did not rely on stage properties it resorted only to the dexterous movement of the hands, making clay balls appear and vanish without any trace. Many typical Chinese magic tricks

which have won high acclaim today, both at home and abroad, have evolved from this. They include "Fairies Planting Beans" (five red beans appear and vanish in the magician's hands), "Three Stars Entering the Cave" (three small parcels of red cloth come and go in the magician's hands), "Passing a Pellet Under the Moon" (a big iron pellet enters the left eye and comes out through the right eye).

With the emergence of gunpowder, fireworks magic and lantern magic arose one after the other. "Fireworks Boxes", "Human Figure Fireworks" (when fireworks were shot into the air, the flare looked like human figures) and "Nine Lanterns" became traditional items and have been handed down to the present.

In addition, there were all sorts of performances of tricks such as "Sword Swallowing" and "Needle Eating", which had a high degree of mystery.

"Spinning Tops" and Other Acts

Most acrobats during the Song Dynasty performed among the common people and roamed here and there to earn a living. There developed a new situation, that of free competition, performers vying with one another professionally. In addition to perfecting their skills on the basis of traditional techniques, performers composed a greater number of new acts to win over their audiences. Many folk games involving muscular skills were improved upon through the painstaking efforts of acrobats and became acrobatic numbers of a special style. For instance, "Spinning Tops", "Pagoda of Bowls", "Balancing in Pairs", "Two-Men Exercises" and "Spinning and Whirling"— were all new numbers appearing during the Song Dynasty.

The modern acrobatic number "Diabolo Play" was evolved from the folk game "Spinning Tops". A "top" is a toy which had its origin in prehistoric times. It is shaped somewhat like an inverted cone, that spins and balances on a point at its apex. At one time it was kept spinning on the ground by means of whipping it. Still later, some persons made the top of bamboo and cut an opening on the top to make it whistle, utilizing the impact of air on it while it was in motion. It was known as the "Ringing Top". During the Song Dynasty it became an acrobatic item. The performers juggled the whirling top on a string, pulling it with two hands and letting it make all sorts of patterns up in the air. At that time it was called "Spinning Tops". It was called "Whistling Bell" during the Ming Dynasty and is known as "Diabolo Play" today. Gradually an increasing number of more difficult diabolo playing skills have been developed, and it has become one of the typical Chinese acrobatic numbers. The origin and development of "Diabolo Play" sheds light on the protracted and complicated process through which a set of successful acrobatic acts has been improved upon.

The image of "Pagoda of Bowls" appeared on stone sculptures as early as during the Han Dynasty, but it was not put on as an acrobatic act until the Song Dynasty, 1,000 years later. It was then called "Feats with Bowls". What is known today as "Plate Spinning", namely, the art of spinning objects such as plates on the tip of a stick, was previously called "Spinning and Whirling".

"Balancing in Pairs" is an acrobatic act in which one performer supports aloft with his hands another performer who is doing handstands, both performers having their hands pressed against each other. In ancient murals can be found pictures of two performers in this position, with one serving as the base while the other performs diverse acrobatic skills. But it has only been described in written records from the Song Dynasty, "Two-Men Exercises" represents another variation of this act in which one performer is supported by another. In this, one acrobat is supported by another who is dancing on his hands or shoulders. The skill of the two above-mentioned items is combined in the acrobatic act "The Pyramid", now in vogue.

"Vocal Mimicry" began very early in China. Its primary form was introduced during the Spring and Autumn and Warring States periods, but it did not emerge as an acrobatic act until the time of the Song Dynasty. The best known example of "Vocal Mimicry" is "A Hundred Birds Chirp". A performer would imitate the sounds of different kinds of birds such as the thrush, lark and cuckoo. This was an act which was often presented at the imperial court.

"Wrestling" was a popular competitive contest during the Zhou and Qin dynasties, and was especially popular during the Song Dynasty when there both male and female wrestlers. An ingenious acrobatic act was developed which was called "Masquerade Wrestling". It was performed in the following fashion: A performer would carry on his back the upper bodies of a pair of puppets of dressed up as opponents. He would bend down and hide himself in the clothes of the puppets and his four limbs would become the two pairs of feet of the puppets. The two puppets then grappled with each other, each trying every way possible to beat the other. At the height of their fierce grapple, the performer would suddenly stand up. Watching this, all the spectators would roar with laughter. This comedy act has been handed down to the present, and is known as "Wrestling Dummies", which still attracts vast audiences.

During the Song Dynasty there were also many kinds of animal shows, quite a number of them with a refreshing flavour of novelty.

The largest animal show was "Elephant Chariot", which was presented at grand celebrations. In this performance, seven elephants driven by seven strongmen in purple garments skilfully knelt, kowtowed and made obeisance. Sometimes, camels also joined in the performance. There were also frequent records of "Monkey Shows" and "Bear Taming".

There were numerous circus acts of training birds and small animals. They had a very rich content, for instance, training crows to play chess and taming a hawfinch to dance with a quail. But the most original and interesting was "Taming Aquatic Animals", a skill which arose during the Song Dynasty. According to the records in the *Gui Xin Zha Shi* (*Random Notes in Guixin Street*) written by Zhou Mi when he lived in Guixin Street, Hangzhou, in the Southern Song Dynasty (1127-1279), the writer saw during his childhood in Lin'an (Hangzhou, capital of the Southern Song Dynasty), a marvellous performance of water creatures, called "Seven Aquatic Games". This was performed by Zhao Xi, a veteran court performer at that time. Zhao Xi put fish, turtles and loaches into a large lacquered vessel filled with fresh water. To the musical accompaniment of a brass gong, any water creature whose name he called would at once swim to the surface of the water. It would also float and dance in the water, wearing a specially devised small mask. The "Seven Aquatic Games" was developed into a high-level performance, both in the design of the act and in the method by which the water creatures were trained.

"Hundred Entertainments" on Water

Jinming Pond in Bianliang, capital of the Northern Song Dynasty, the West Lake and the Qiantang River in Lin'an, capital of the Southern Song Dynasty, were all good Places for sports and amusements on water. People, during the Song Dynasty, were especially fond of watching performances on water while they were boating on the lake or watching the spectacular scene of the high tides at the mouth of the Qiantang River. Many acrobatic performances were interspersed with other types of entertainment. The most representative of these were "Swinging on Water" and "Sporting with Tides".

"Swinging on Water" was a frequently held sport during the Northern Song Dynasty.

Tall swinging frames were erected on the bows of two exquisitely carved boats on the bank of the Jinming Pond. To the beating of drums, acrobats on the stern would first perform "Gymnastics on a Pole" and then "Brandishing Flags". At the climax of the performance they got on the swings, and in succession went into full swing. When the swings rose as high as the frames they suddenly let loose the ropes and went up into the air and, relying on propulsion from the swings, they turned somersaults in the air and plunged into the water, each taking a different posture. It was thrilling to the audience and the scene created was a picture of beauty.

"Sporting with Tides" during the Southern Song Dynasty was even more spectacular. Every year on the 18th day of the eighth lunar month, three days after the Mid-Autumn Festival, at the time when the ebb and flow of the tides on the Qiantang River were most manifest, nearly all residents of Lin'an came out from the city to watch the rushing in of the high tides at the mouth of the Qiantang River. Performers displayed their skills in the tempestuous tides. In groups ranging from dozens to a hundred, with each performer holding different-sized flags or parasols with floral designs, they dived into the crest of the water. They sported with the flags in the midst of the waves. To be able to keep the flags from being moistened testified to the performers' superb skills, bravery and wisdom. One outstanding performer, named Li Waining, was good at presenting puppet shows on water. He devised an act called "Hundred Entertainments on Water", making use of water power to manoeuvre the puppets and make them perform acrobatics while on the water. His unique design aroused the attention of the spectators and his name was mentioned by many writers.

"Variety Shows" During the Yuan Dynasty

During the Yuan Dynasty (1279-1368), which was founded by the Mongols after they unified the whole country, there arose severe class discrepancies and national contradictions. The Yuan government prescribed that the commoners were not allowed to keep iron utensils, to practise martial skills or to raise horses. These stipulations made it impossible for many acrobatic acts to be performed and so there were only a few occasional performances, called "Variety Shows".

The court acrobatic troupe of the Yuan Dynasty was very small in size, having only 150 performers. It was under the supervision of the office for training music and dance performers and put on very simple performances. According to the accounts in the *Travels of Marco Polo*, the Venetian traveller had watched an acrobatic performance after feasting at the imperial court of Emperor Shi Zu (Kublai Khan, reigning 1260-1294). The programme included handstands and juggling with hands. *Xu Wen Xian Tong Kao* (*Sequel to Studies in Ancient Bibliographies*) written by Wang Qi and completed in 1586 during the Ming Dynasty, also describes acrobatic performances witnessed during the Yuan Dynasty. The writer informs us that, "performances for the emperor included 'Variety Shows', 'Pole Balancing' (performers on two poles exchanging their positions), 'Rope Walking', 'Juggling with the Feet' and 'Hiding Tricks' ". Judging by the written records, the Yuan Dynasty carried on the acrobatic tradition of the Song Dynasty, without adding anything new.

Folk acrobats had few opportunities to perform. Some were adle to take part in the performances of the rising *zaju*, the celebrated Yuan Dynasty drama, where they could perform stunts of "Turning Somersaults" in acrobatic fighting as well as "Brandishing Big Flags" and "Walking on Stilts". Some of them were masters of excellent skills and there was reported a thrilling presentation of turning 200 somersaults in one stretch in some of the plays.

Those acrobats who roamed the streets and lanes could only put on some brief acts to earn a living, although some of them also had extraordinary skills. According to an account in *Nan Cun Chuo Geng Lu* (*Talks in the Intervals of Ploughing at Nancun*), a book which records the anecdotes, laws and regulations, cultural and current affairs of the Yuan Dynasty, the writer saw an acrobat in Hangzhou perform an act with seven trained tortoises of varying sizes. Each tortoise voluntarily climbed onto the back of another, forming a pyramid. The tortoise on the top raised its body with its tail curled up, resembling a small pagoda. This act was called "A Pagoda of Tortoises". There was another performance of trained frogs. The largest of nine frogs squatted on a small block and the eight others were deployed on its left and right. The large frog croaked once and the eight others followed suit. When the large one croaked several times, so did the eight others. It looked as if the large frog were a teacher training his students. Finally, each small frog came in front of the "Elder" and bowed before making an exit. This act was called "Frog Preaching". There is evidence that this performance continued to be presented as late as during the Qing Dynasty (1644-1911).

6. Out of the Rulers' Favour, But Still Popular

(A.D. 1368-1949)

Ming (1368-1644) and Qing (1644-1911) were China's last two feudal dynasties. After the Opium War in 1840, owing to the corruption and incompetence of the Qing government, China had actually degraded into a semi-feudal and semi-colonial society. Feudal relationships decreased and forms of capitalist production steadily increased as the number of people in the cities gradually grew. Acrobatic art was faced with the following conditions: on the one hand, the vast number of working people, the townspeople in particular, loved to have acrobatics with its long historical tradition, to enrich their cultural life. They appreciated its presentation of physical prowess and muscular skills of the human body. On the other hand, the rulers continued to hold the prejudices prevalent among the ruling class of the Song Dynasty, and regarded acrobatics as shows not appealing to refined taste, and therefore discriminated against it. Consequently, Ming and Qing dynasty acrobats gave most of their performany among the common people, the major forms being open-air shows at the Qingming Festival (a traditional Chinese festival mainly for paying respect to ancestral tombs, which falls around April 5 each year), when people made excursions to the countryside in spring, shows at religious parades, and demonstrations of skills by strolling per-

formers. The only exceptions were "Humorous Shows About Daily Life", "Horsemanship" and "Ice Games" which were presented at the imperial court during the Ming and Qing dynasties. The latter two portrayed the life of the minority peoples.

Ming and Qing dynasty acrobatics was entirely different from that of the preceding dynasties in that it had its base among the ordinary people. Also, with the formation and development of China as a unified, multi-national country, Ming and Qing dynasty acrobatics covered a greater number of gymnastic skills from nationalities other than the Hans, and the performances became more varied and colourful. During the 500 years of performing among the people, Ming and Qing dynasty acrobatics began to reflect the interests of the people, and so the performances were designed to be better seen by spectators from four sides of the arena, and new acrobatic items were constantly brought forth. They were no longer as elegant as those of the Song Dynasty. Feats of physical prowess were added and they were more difficult to perform. Hence the shows became more splendid and held greater attraction for the spectators. Acrobatic art and other branches of the performing arts began to influence one another. This promoted the development of other branches of art while at the same time acrobatics itself blazed new trails. For instance, Peking Opera and traditional local operas borrowed from acrobatics, so that striking a pose on the stage and acrobatic fighting in Chinese classical drama reflected its special style. Acrobatic acts also became shorter and more flexible so that they varied with the time, place and conditions according to the requirements of the performances. Hence a good effect was achieved.

In particular, we should point out that the acrobats of the Ming and Qing dynasties gave touring performances, rain or shine. Even when undergoing harsh conditions, they brought the traditional art to the cities and the countryside, and to remote, out-of-the-way places. They contributed to the spreading and development of the culture of the Chinese nation and paved the way for the flowering of contemporary acrobatics.

"Humorous Shows About Daily Life"

As acrobatics had a very low status during the Yuan Dynasty, the imperial court of the Ming and Qing dynasties did not have large-sized troupes. Although some new creations were performed for the court, they were only fragmentary.

The Ming Dynasty had a very small Royal Theatre, and that was only for the entertainment of the royal house. Humorous shows about daily life were often presented at the imperial court. They resembled both a group dance of the Song Dynasty and the Yuan Dynasty drama, and contained elements of both acrobatics and magic. According to what has been written in *Ming Gong Shi* (*History of the Ming Court*), humorous shows about daily life accompanied by bell ringing and drum beating were presented in about 100 acts, each act with about a dozen performers. The content was both refined and popular. The essential element was their funny ending, usually in the form of jokes. Each act was initiated with a presentation of flags accompanied by gongs and drums. The acts portrayed scenes of daily life, including family life. Merchants and craftsmen in towns and at markets, as well as aspects of life such as fraud, swindle and lawsuits were depicted. A witty presen-

tation was emphasized, and most of the shows were humorous. Acrobatic and magic shows were a part of the performances.

"Picture of Lantern Festival at the New Year" (Colour plate 7), a huge scroll painting in the collection of Beijing's Palace Museum, depicts a scene of streets and market places laid at the imperial court of the Ming Dynasty for the festival of the lunar New Year. Setting off fire crackers and displaying varied and colourful lanterns, as was common among the people, are shown in the picture which was painted in the 21st year of the Chenghua reign (A. D. 1485). A long section of the scroll depicts acrobatic performances.

In the painting Emperor Xian Zong (reigning 1465-1487), in informal attire, sits under a canopy in a palace hall with attendants standing at both sides. A string of palace lanterns are hung up in the hall, presenting a sumptuous atmosphere. Four persons are standing in the hall. One person is announcing the programme to the emperor, and another person is giving directions in the hall.

In the foreground of the picture an actor, on top of a table, is standing on the head of another performer, doing a balancing act.

In front of the table is a magician performing a magic show called "Tubes" (two or three hollow bamboo tubes are placed one on top of the other, and wine, dishes or a monkey is conjured out of them). Stage properties are displayed on the table. There are four musicians at his side, performing musical accompaniment with rapt attention.

In the centre of the painting can be seen two different forms of juggling with feet going on at the same time. In one group, a performer is lying on his back on the table and with his feet he is juggling a heavy cart wheel on which another performer is standing. "Juggling a Child" is an act being performed by another group. An acrobat, with fast moving feet, is juggling a child up into the air. Gong and drum accompaniment is played at their side, while an assistant performer, probably "guaranteeing their safety", watches their movements.

The description of "Jumping Through a Hoop" presents a more graceful picture of movements. A performer, wearing only pants, and with the upper part of his body and feet naked, jumps through a large hoop on a table. In front of the hoop is another performer, in the same style of attire, who has already jumped through the hoop. Behind the hoop is another acrobat performing a handstand. Thus the picture shows a series of continuous group movements in the performance of "Jumping Through a Hoop".

In the painting can be seen a huge coloured canopy, hung at the back. Eight Taoist immortals are embroidered on the canopy, where there are also palace lanterns. Beneath the canopy, a thrilling "Feat of Juggling a Pole" is being performed. An acrobat can be seen lying on a table, juggling a long pole with his feet. On the pole is a performer waving a coloured flag. The action resembles the last movement of today's feat of juggling called "Scattered Ladder" (with all the rungs of the ladder falling off and the acrobat displaying his skills on the ladder posts).

A "Lion Dance" is also depicted in the painting. One man is leading a man masquerading as a lion on whose back is riding another man. It is a parade-like performance. In addition to about a dozen acrobatic items the painting also portrays "Lanterns with Revolving Figures" (lanterns with papercut figures of men, animals, etc. revolving when the lanterns are lit), "Setting Off Fireworks", "Dressing Up as a Peddler", and other amusements. Only a limited number of performers, assistants, bands of percussion music and reed-pipes and pedestrian spectators appear in the painting, but it offers a true picture of a "Humorous Show About Daily Life" which illustrates the customs of the common people.

Acrobatics at the Imperial Court of the Qing Dynasty

Because there were many acrobats in the troops of peasants during their uprisings at the end of the Ming Dynasty, the rulers of the early Qing Dynasty hated, killed and exiled many acrobats and did not permit them to form troupes. The Qing Dynasty court had no pure acrobatic performances. Later, the Qing Dynasty rulers brought back a number of the acrobatic acts of some of the minority nationalities after they had quelled the rebellions in frontier areas. These included "Brass Wire Walking", "Gymnastics on a Pole" and "Twirling Bowls" of the Uygurs and Huis and the "Group Dance of Somersaults" of the Koreans and the "Lion Dance" of the Tibetan style in the area of

Greater Jinchuan (present-day Jinchuan in Sichuan Province).

"Brass Wire Walking" was the Uygur style of rope walking. Its advantage was to change rope walking into brass wire walking, and was the original form of today's wire walking. It involved superb skills. In some performances a person walked up along a slanting wire and then took off his boots when at the top. Some performers trod on a brass plate while walking on the wire, and some walked on stilts on the wire. All of them jumped, pranced and performed somersaults while walking on the wire.

When the Manchus swept down from Northeast China and entered the Shanhai Pass to dominate the rest of the country, they made Beijing their capital. They brought with them the favourite traditional games of their own nationality. Some games had a rich acrobatic flavour such as "Wrestling" (Colour plate 8) and "Dance of Brave Warriors", an animal masquerade group dance. This dance portrays 40 warriors of the "Eight Banners" (military administrative organizations of the Manchu nationality during the Qing Dynasty) chasing after 16 men wearing masks and animal pelts and masquerading as fierce beasts, making somersaults in succession, performing leaps and practising archery on horseback. The dance represented the bravery of the young men of the "Eight Banners" at the entry of the Manchus into the interior of China.

"Horsemanship" was an item more popular among the Manchus and the Mongolians (Colour plate 9). *Qing Wen Xian Tong Kao* (*Studies in Qing Dynasty Bibliographies*) records that 120 experts in horsemanship and archery were selected in the 12th year of the Qianlong reign (A. D. 1747). Jiang Shiquan, a scholar during the early Qing Dynasty, called horsemanship "acrobatic skills on horseback". He said that according to an old Mongolian custom an annual horsemanship demonstration was held at the imperial court during the festival of the lunar New Year. It was conventionally held at the same time as the display of lanterns. The demonstration began with a display of horsemanship. Some riders galloped while standing with one foot or both feet on horseback. Some riders exchanged horses, each jumping to the other's horse. Following the exchange of horses were breathtaking movements such as posing in the form of a human pagoda on horseback. The horsemanship went on until sunset, at which time many performers waved coloured lanterns and sang while standing in neat formations. The formations were repeatedly changing, grouping the lanterns into the characters "Long Live Peace". At this time many fireworks were set off, making a thunderous noise and brightening the sky with light. It appeared as if thousands of red fish were jumping and prancing in a sea of clouds.

Ice sports, which were performed outside the Shanhai Pass, were another of the folk games which had rich content. The Qing court called them "Ice Games", and they had a more distinctive national characteristic. Coupled with traditional archery, these sports involved high muscular skills.

The Eight Banners selected 200 crack skaters to receive training for "Ice Games" in the 10th lunar month of every year. The performance began at the imperial court after the Winter Solstice, which falls during the last 10 days of the 11th lunar month of approximately the last 10 days of December.

The sport would begin with a contest of speed skating, and a huge flag would be planted 1.5 kilometres away. With the firing of the gun, the contestants started and whoever first got hold of the huge flag won a prize. Immediately afterwards was "Snatching a Ball" which resembled a Rugby football contest, but was done on ice skates. Soldiers played the game in two teams, one on the left and the other on the right. The left team was clad in red and the right team in yellow. A royal guardman fiercely kicked a leather ball to the centre, and the soldiers vyed with one another in snatching it. The one who had got it threw it and the ball snatching started again. Sometimes a soldier got the ball and it was snatched again, or he fell on the ice and leapt high to snatch it back.

"Shooting the Balls" was an item very similar to acrobatics. More than 200 standard-bearers and over 400 archers in an array of Eight Banners wound its way like a floating dragon on a skating rink. An archway of flags hung with a "Celestial Ball" and an "Earth Ball" were put up near the emperor's throne. Archers shot the balls with their bows and arrows while skating. Whoever shot down the balls was the winner. A picture of the "Ice Games" was stored in the imperial palace of the Qing Dynasty. Apart from the above-mentioned games, it also depicts many other acrobatic movements on the skating rink.

A Spring Outing

The Qingming Festival is a marvellous time for enjoying spring scenery, and in ancient times people practised the custom of having a spring outing. *Xi Hu You Lan Zhi Yu* (*Random Notes on West Lake Excursions*), written by Tian Rucheng of the Ming Dynasty, describes how Hangzhou was bustling with activity at the time of the Qingming Festival: "The vicinity of the Su Dyke lay under the shade of luxuriant willow twigs and verdancy was interspersed with pink peach blossoms. Many shows and games were presented for people's entertainment such as Rope Walking, Riding on Valiant Horses, Juggling Coins or Cymbals, Spreading Sand, Swallowing Knives, Spitting Fire, Jumping Through Hoops, Turning Somersaults, and Spinning Plates, as well as insect and ant masquerade shows" (Colour plates 10, 11, 12, 13 & 14).

There were also folk performances with astonishing feats of high acrobatic skills. The same book describes "Gymnastics on a Pole" at the fair at the Yousheng Temple in Hangzhou on the third day of the third lunar month. A 10-metre-high pole was hoisted in the centre of the courtyard. The performers went up and down the pole, doing such breathtaking movements as "Sparrow-Hawk Turns Somersaults", "Golden Cockerel Stands on One Foot", "Zhong Kui Gazes Ahead While Shading His Forehead and Holding the Pole Under One Arm" and "Jade Hare Pestles Medicine in a Mortar". Spectators were thrilled and astonished at so many changes and variations.

The most lively acrobatic festival at the time of Qingming Festival during the Ming Dynasty was in the vicinity of the Gaoliang Bridge on the outskirts of the capital, Beijing. There were many handicraft stalls and peddlers carrying hot delicious snacks on shoulder poles. Some roaming acrobats offered outdoor shows on a piece of vacant ground. Some performed singly and others staged shows with their apprentices, sons and daughters.

Quite a number of acrobatic acts performed at the time of spring outings were popular for their refreshing novelty. These included "Gymnastics on a Pole", "Turning Somersaults", "Jumping Through Hoops on the Ground", "Turning Somersaults on a Table", "Equestrian Skills" and "Target

Shooting with Bow and Pellets". Most of these numbers had not appeared until the Ming Dynasty.

"Gymnastics on a Pole" was devised by improving upon "Pole Balancing", thus freeing the performer on the pole from a shaky, swaying situation. A pole was planted in the ground and fastened with ropes on four sides. The acrobat could go up and down and do all sorts of gymnastic movements on the fixed pole without worrying that the pole would fall down. This resulted in an increase of rapid, vigorous movements.

"Jumping Through Hoops on the Ground" was a new item developed from an ancient piece known as "Rushing Through a Narrow Space". It turned an ancient flitting, breathtaking movement into an integrated set of skills done with effortless grace.

"Turning Somersaults on a Table" was an item in which a performer turned somersaults in diverse postures on the topmost of three tables piled one on the other, and then leapt down to the ground with perfect balance. The most fascinating movement was one in which the performer started by waving a pair of loops, one in each hand. He then swooped down, performing a somersault and landing on the ground, with the loops hung around his neck. This was the original form of the traditional acrobatic act, "Three Tables and Nine Bowls".

"Target Shooting with Bow and Pellets" was a miraculous skill appearing at this time. A performer with a bow in his hand shot a clay pellet up into the air. While the pellet was falling down, he shot the second pellet to hit it. The two pellets would break into smithereens in mid-air. There were many other difficult acts using the bow such as shooting from behind and hitting a pellet on the top of a child's head from a distance and two performers shooting at each other, making the pellets meet in mid-air.

The last item on the programme, at the time of spring outings at the Gaoliang Bridge, was setting off fireworks in the evening. It was a thrilling scene, having many fireworks explode in the sky high above the water's surface.

To do acrobatic feats during spring outings was a custom which came into being during the Ming Dynasty when many new acrobatic numbers emerged. All of them were devised and refined by wandering performers during the stormy 100 years which followed the Song Dynasty (960-1279). Short flexible items became predominant and have formed the mainstream of modern acrobatics.

Strolling Religious Processions

The strolling religious procession was an ancient form of theatrical performance especially popular during the Ming and Qing dynasties. These performances differed somewhat from that temple fairs of the Southern and Northern Dynasties in that they were spontaneous acrobatic parades of the common people who gave performances. The people offered prayers for a rich harvest and to avert disasters, and the strolling religious procession was one way they prayed. The processions also contained lively entertainment, and so throngs of people participated in them. The rulers encouraged these religious processions as so to take the blame off themselves for famines and dire poverty of the people. Consequently, acrobats found a regular source of livelihood in such religious processions while the fans of acrobatics enjoyed the artistic presentations.

According to the records in *Wu She Pian* (*Informal Essays on Theatrical Society*) written by Wang Zhideng, there were excerpts from drama in the masquerade processions, for example, from the "Conqueror of Chu", "General Guan Yu Goes Alone to a Rendezvous Carrying a Heavy Halberd" and "Eight Immortals Celebrate Their Birthdays". Some performers dressed themselves up as Guan Yin (the Goddess of Mercy), the God Erlang, and the Eighteen Buddhist Arhats. Some masqueraded as ancient personages such as Jiang the Venerable (who reportedly lived in the 11th century B. C.), poet Li Bai and the Eighteen Court Scholars. There were also characters from the life of the townspeople. All characters in the procession were either seated or standing on a large wooden board, carried by others, hence it was described as being a "Platform-Carrying Procession".

There were also acrobatic acts presented such as, "Gymnastics on a Pole", "Jumping Through a Gate of Knives", "Horsemanship", "Rope Walking", "Guangdong Lion" and puppet shows. These traditional numbers were interspersed in the programme (Figures 55 & 56).

During the Qing Dynasty, strolling religious processions became more prevalent and included a greater number of acrobatic performances. Beginning at the time of the Qianlong reign (1735-1796), there were fairs in the nature of bazaars on ordinary days and apart from the religious festivals.

Temple fairs represented another type of activity. Some were temple fairs at religious festivals, for offering incense and praying for good fortune, and others were bazaar-like temple fairs on ordinary days. The latter had a richer folk flavour, with a greater number of people attending. Performers at a temple fair put up large or small tents for performances, to attract the spectators. Apart from professional performers, there were also numerous amateur acrobats and some young Manchus of the "Eight Banners",

55. "Juggling a Heavy Load with the Feet" in the "Picture of a Strolling Religious Procession" from the Qing Dynasty.

56. "Folk horsemanship" in a New Year picture in woodcut from the Qing Dynasty.

who took part in the performances of strolling religious processions or temple fairs.

The strolling procession proceeded in a regular order and there were certain persons in charge of it, each with a particular job. "Head of the procession" walked in the forefront with another person carrying a flag. Some other persons superintended miscellaneous affairs on the way. Performers were called "experts". Each group of performances was followed by an orchestra and the performances were arranged in a certain sequence. The "Picture of a Strolling Religious Procession" in the collection of the renowned Peking Opera actor, Cheng Yanqiu, vividly portrays the scene of a strolling procession during the Qing Dynasty. In this picture can be seen "Flying Tridents" at the front of the procession, which consists of a five-member group masquerading as "Five

57. "Waving the Central Banner" in the "Picture of a Strolling Religious Procession" from the Qing Dynasty.

Ghosts Tease the Judge of Hell". While marching ahead, they brandish three-pronged tridents, sometimes throwing them up into the air, sometimes swirling them around their bodies. This makes the spectators dodge aside so as to have more space, therefore, this item was also called "Opening the Way". In its wake is "Waving the Central Banner" (Figure 57). An expert with a commanding presence hoists an eight-metre long bamboo pole on which is hung a huge banner with big characters reading, "Wishing You a Long Life", written on it as the hallmark of the whole religious procession. The principal movement of "Waving the Central Banner" is throwing the banner high up, with the long pole always dropping down vertically. The performer catches the banner with his forehead, nose bridge, the back of his head, elbow or knee. Bells are put at the tip of the pole. When the procession goes through the ornamental archway in the middle of the street, the banner cannot fit under it. The carrier of the banner is usually not willing

to lower the banner to pass under the archway. Instead, he exerts great effort to hoist the banner pole high over the archway, and he himself runs fast under the archway, catching the pole on the other side. This movement of vitality and daring is greatly appreciated by the thousands of spectators who vye with one another to get a glimpse of the act.

The performances following "Waving the Central Banner" could be arranged in any order. The following categories were often seen:

Acts performed with stage props made of coloured silks such as the "Lion Dance" (Figure 58), which was symbolic of good luck. During the late Qing Dynasty most Beijing performers of the "Lion Dance" were those who specialized in the trade of putting up awnings of reed mats. Two performers masqueraded as a large lion called, "Senior Lion". One man dressed as a small lion called, "Junior Lion". Whenever it crossed a bridge, the Senior Lion suspended itself

58. "Lion Dance" in the "Picture of a Strolling Religious Procession" from the Qing Dynasty.

59. "Feats on a Bar" in the "Picture of a Strolling Religious Procession" from the Qing Dynasty.

on the bridge with its head downward and performed the movement "Sporting with Water", bending its body close to the water. Whenever it met a flagpole or the pillar of a pavilion, the "Junior Lion" did gymnastics on the pole or pillar.

Such acts as a "Small Cart Show", "Rowing an Imaginary Boat" and "A Donkey Ride" often appeared in the strolling procession. A performer slipped into a cart, a boat or the head and tail of a donkey made of coloured silks and danced while carrying the cart, boat or donkey around. An orchestra following behind played accompaniment in perfect harmony with the performer. They presented items with simple plots such as "A Big-Headed Monk Teases a Young Girl" and "A Bride Returns to Her Parents' Home".

Feats of physical prowess and martial arts could also be seen in the procession, such as "Thousand-Pound Rock". A performer, acting as the base, lay on the ground with his face up. With his feet, he supported a stone barbell with several other acrobats performing handstands and forming a human pyramid on it. In another of such feats of physical prowess, a performer was displaying the art of handling a barbell, twirling it around his body and shoulders. This was called "Flying Stones in Five Manoeuvres".

When an acrobat performed "Juggling Stone Locks", he did "Lifting Up", "Throwing It High Up", "Juggling into Each Other's Hands", "Balancing It on the Head" and "Supporting It with the Elbow" while he was walking. The stone lock weighed between 10 and 30 kilogrammes. "Juggling Bricks" was lighter but involved more complicated movements. Experts juggled stone locks in ordinary times and bricks in strolling processions.

"Five-Tiger Clubs" and "Shaolin Clubs" represented acrobatic fighting of the martial arts. "Five-Tiger Club" experts dressed up as such historical figures as Zhao Kuangyin, Zheng Ziming and Chai Rong. Chai Rong met the five brothers of the Dong family nicknamed "Five Tigers" when passing a bridge. He fought the Dong brothers in a fierce battle.   There were also performances depicting episodes in the *Outlaws of the Marsh*, a famous classical Chinese novel.   They often used real weapons.

Gymnastic feats performed in the procession were mainly "Feats on a Bar" (Figure 59), "Juggling Jars" and "Walking on Stilts". "Feats on a Bar" was new and emerged during the Qing Dynasty.   Performers changed from climbing vertical poles into performing stunts on a horizontal bar.   The feats included spinning, and suspending on the bar. During the middle of the Qing Dynasty a lame performer, named Tian, was famed for spinning on the horizontal bar like lightning, despite his handicap.   In a strolling procession experts brought the bar and supporting

frame with them and when they came to open grounds, they rigged up the bar for a group performance.

Experts walked on stilts dressed up as fishermen or as the White Snake or the Green Snake who had transformed themselves into beautiful women from mythological stories. Walking on three-metre-high stilts, they performed the movements of advancing, retreating, leaping, prancing, doing the splits and whirling.   They leapt high slopes or flights of steps (Figure 60).

The strolling procession was gigantic and presented almost too many items for the spectators to take in.   Many acrobatic numbers from those processions continue to survive on the stage today.

60. Photograph of a strolling religious procession in the Qing Dynasty

"Celebratory Hall Performances" and
"Roadside Performances"

In addition to strolling processions and temple fairs, there were two other main forms by which acrobats sold their art to earn a

living, namely, "Celebratory Hall Performances" and "Roadside Performances".

"Celebratory Hall Performances" refer to

the occasions, sometimes lasting several days, when a wealthy and influential family celebrated the birthday or wedding of one of its members and invited opera stars, ballad singers or acrobats to their home to present performances. The programme and festivities usually consisted of items symbolizing good luck. As the performances were presented on a makeshift stage erected in a hall or a courtyard, they were called "Celebratory Hall Performances". Among the acts presented in today's performances of "Traditional-Style Conjuring" is one called "Conjuring in a Hall" because it is taken from the "Celebratory Hall Performances" of former times. When performing conjuring acts, magicians excelled in tricks using the movements of the waist, and could withdraw from their clothing 13 platters of fruit and pastries for the birthday celebration as well as other large-size objects such as a vase with vertical flanges symbolizing "Peace Across the Land" and "Pearl-Adorned Lantern" (Colour plate 15). In the final conjuring act, the magician took off his long robe and appeared in close-fitting attire. He then turned a somersault and two bowls of water instantly appeared. This was the well-known trick, "A Moon Comes out of a Somersault".

The 18th century scholar Ji Yun in his *Yue Wei Cao Tang Bi Ji* (*Notes of the Yuewei Hermitage*) recalled the magic show he had seen during his childhood in his grandfather's home. It was a "Celebratory Hall Performance" in approximately 1734. Ji Yun was the editor-in-chief of the *Si Ku Quan Shu* (*The Imperial Library of Qianlong*) at the time of the Qianlong reign during the Qing Dynasty. He said:

After performing such brief magic acts as the "Vanishing of a Gold Goblet" and "A Cup Comes Out of the Ground", a magician took a large bowl of fish from the banquet table and threw it up into the air. It vanished in an instant. The host and the guests asked him to conjure it back. He said: "Im-

possible. The fish is in a drawer of a desk in your study. Go and get it back yourself!" When they went to the study, they saw that the drawer was too flat and narrow to contain such a large fish bowl. They did not believe the magician's words. They pulled open the drawer, and to their surprise the fish was on a flat plate which had originally been put elsewhere and in which there had been a fingered citron (called Buddha's hand). When they looked at the spot where the fingered citron was placed, they found the fruit in the large fish bowl.

When a magician went to a person's house, he needed to make the best use of the situation for his conjury. It was necessary to combine a clever design prepared beforehand and a well rehearsed instantaneous action. Without superb skill and abundant experience, he could not succeed. For instance, the removal of a bowl of fish and pitting it into the family's desk was meticulously arranged. The spectators were spellbound with amazement.

"Roadside Performance" was a form of performing art which began during the Song and Yuan dynasties, when strolling performers put up stalls on street corners for magic and acrobatic shows. They were seen more frequently during the Ming and Qing dynasties. At that time many performers came to major cities and gradually regular performance arenas were established. For example, during the Jiaqing reign (1796-1820) at the time of the Qing Dynasty, all sorts of shows such as "Playing Flower-Drums" (a folk dance popular in the Yangtze valley), "Jumping Through Hoops", "Comic Dialogue" and "Magic Acts" were presented along the roadside from the vicinity of the Confucian Temple to the Provincial Examination Centre (the site where provincial civil examinations were held in feudal dynasties). Each visitor could find his favourite form of entertainment (Colour plates 16, 17, 18 & 19).

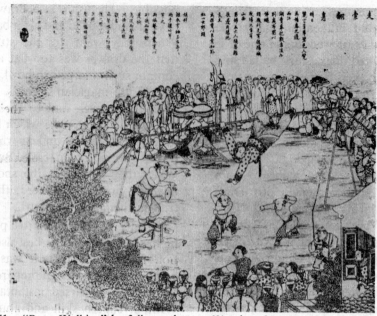

61. "Rope Walking" by folk acrobats — Woodcut from the Qing Dynasty.

Li Dou of the Qing Dynasty wrote about the performances on the bank of the Slender West Lake in his book *Yang Zhou Hua Fang Lu* (*Notes on a Pleasure Boat in Yang-zhou*). He wrote: "Variety shows, coming from all places, gather on a dyke". There were acrobatic performances of "Feats on Poles", "Rope Walking", "Swinging Meteors" and "Swallowing Swords" (Figure 61). There were also interesting magic acts using fire, such as "Taking Fire from a Wall" and "Lighting Lanterns on a Wall" when a performer lit several lanterns at once with a single breath. The art of *qi gong* (traditional Chinese deep breathing exercise) was also used, which made the performer remain unscathed when another man stabbed him with a knife. "Windmill Display" was an act in which a woman performer, seated at the centre of a horizontally placed large cart wheel, was unharmed while the wheel was revolving. "Rice Winnowing" was another act. In this one a performer with a basket in his hands winnowed while walking forward

and did not spill even one grain of rice. All these acts demonstrated the skills of farm work. In addition, there were a dazzling display of other magic tricks including "Spurting Water", "Picking Beans" and "Conjuring Coins". The highlight was "Waving the Central Banner" by a 90-year-old performer who was balancing a 50-kilogramme heavy bamboo pole more than 10 metres long on his head. These fine performances attracted the visitors on passing pleasure boats and they eagerly gave money for the entertainments.

Many cities had spots similar to the vicinity of the Confucian Temple in Nanjing and the bank of the Slender West Lake in Yangzhou, where many performers demonstrated their skills to eke out a living. For instance, Tianqiao (the Heavenly Bridge) in the southern part of Beijing, "San Bu Guan" in Tianjin, and the Town God's Temple Market (a shopping bazaar today) in Shanghai (Figures 62 & 63). There were curtained-off grounds, one after another, and

one theatrical tent after another at these spots. Performers did conjuring tricks, brandished steel tridents, juggled stone barbells, balanced jars, played diabolos, narrated stories and sang arias, year after year. Performers vyed with one another in presenting all sorts of shows and bringing forth something novel and unusual. Countless spectators came to such spots, therefore, many peddlers followed suit and tea booths and taverns also opened there. After a time these spots became well-known places for amusement. They examplified the tradition of the "Curtained-Off Arenas" of the Song Dynasty. Many performers stayed there all year long. They practised hard at their skills and with their sons, nephews and apprentices, gave several shows a day. As years went by, many became expert acrobats with unique skills.

62. Acrobats sold their art at Tianqiao (the Heavenly Bridge) in the southern part of Beijing before liberation.

A number of new-style live performance amusement parks appeared in Shanghai and Wuhan at the end of the 19th century. For

63. Acrobatic performances in Shanghai's Yu-yuan Garden — Woodcut from the Qing Dynasty.

the purpose of making profit, some speculating merchants built indoor amusement parks and provided all sorts of entertainment and performances, tea houses, restaurants and places for playing games. For instance, the "Great World" in Shanghai, the "New World" in Wuhan and the "Popular Amusement Park" in Chongqing.

Private amusement park owners employed performers at very low "regular pay". Those employed included actors from many acrobatic companies and troupes as well as those who performed acrobatic and magic acts without being affiliated to any troupe. They made these performers present shows all day long to attract thousands of spectators. Thus the owners reaped unfair gains while the performers in the amusement parks led a very miserable life, fleeced by the exploitation and oppression of the capitalists, local ruffians and villains. But many perform-

ers had no other way to earn a livelihood so they usually stayed on in such an amusement park from three to five years. Some stayed as long as 10 to 20 years. Although they lived in poor circumstances, it was more stable than working as itinerant performers. Making use of these stable conditions, many of them practised with painstaking effort to perfect their skills and eventually became famous actors with great accomplishments. For instance, two performers, a brother and sister, named Pan, and Mo Feixian, of today's Shanghai Acrobatic Tropue; Chen Laben, a famous clown, and Chen Liben, an animal tamer, of today's China Acrobatic Troupe, as well as pole-balancing expert, Du Shaoyi, of today's Chongqing Acrobatic Troupe have all come from the amusement parks. It might be said that amusement parks stored up talents for the development of contemporary acrobatic art.

Innovative Acrobatic Acts

Selling one's art as a performer became such a widespread practice that it encouraged acrobatic professionals of the Qing Dynasty to bring forth something new at all times. For example, "Feats on Leather Straps" (Figure 64) was a new gymnastic skill evolved from the art of "Gymnastics on a Pole". During the performances several leather straps hung down from the upper end of a framework supported by wooden bars. A performer leapt up from the ground and, taking the leather straps in his hand, twisted his waist and suspended him in the air. Combining strength and dexterity, supple grace and firmness, and interspersing rapid and slow tempos, the performance represented a brand new style.

During the Qing Dynasty feats of juggling

with the hands covered an ever increasing variety. "Flying Trident" was developed

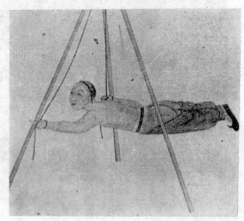

64. Feats on Leather Straps — Genre painting from the Qing Dynasty.

from the art of brandishing clubs and spears. With his upper body naked and manoeuvring the muscular strength of his arms and upper body, a performer wielded a three-pronged trident equipped with resonant iron rings so that it rang melodiously. This act displayed the health and beauty of the human body and its power of control.

"Baton Play" was another light, graceful form of juggling with the hands. Nimble and ingenious, it was an acrobatic act evolved from "Da Lian Xiang", a folk show in which the performer sang and danced while juggling two batons threaded with bronze coins. A performer with a slender baton in each hand used them to poke a third baton which sometimes twirled, sometimes nodded, but never fell down. *Di Jing Sui Shi Ji Sheng* (*Wonders of Fine Seasons in the Capital*), written by Pan Rongsheng in the 23rd year of the Qianlong reign (A. D. 1758), contains a description of this act, recounting that the performance was permeated with singing, dancing and acrobatic fighting.

In the act, "Billiard on the Head", a performer wearing a leather bowl on his head juggled a small wooden ball while in diverse postures and the wooden ball would infallibly drop into the leather bowl. The performance was refreshing and humorous.

During the Ming Dynasty there were acts which displayed feats of juggling with the feet, for instance, juggling heavy objects, children, and long poles. During the Qing Dynasty, among the attractions in the art of juggling with the feet were also "Juggling Jars" and "Kicking a Shuttlecock". These new acts were created from Song Dynasty juggling skills. By changing balls into porcelain jars and shuttlecocks, they better demonstrated the marvellous and difficult gymnastic skills of the Qing Dynasty performers.

The shuttlecock, used in acrobatics, was made with a feather weighted with a bronze coin beneath it. This performance depends entirely on gymnastic skill to be able to kick from diverse postures. According to a description by Li Diaoyuan, a drama theoretician and a man of letters of the Qing Dynasty, Beijing shuttlecock experts could "kick" a shuttlecock not only with their feet, but also with their head, forehead, mouth, nose, shoulders, abdomen and back. A person could kick against several persons. A person could make the shuttlecock twirl around his body without dropping it. During the late Qing Dynasty, Beijing residents were especially fond of group shuttlecock kicking. People would stand in a circle, kicking and passing the shuttlecock to one another without dropping it. After catching the shuttlecock, a person could display his skills by kicking in a series and variety of patterns.

65. Front cover of the book *Xiang Ling Zhi Nan* (*Guide to Shuttlecock Kicking*) written during the Qing Dynasty.

It became very popular and there appeared such masters as "Shuttlecock Tan", who introduced many new methods of kicking and wrote the *Xiang Ling Zhi Nan* (*Guid to Shuttle-cock Kicking*) which has been handed down to the present (Figure 65).

"Juggling Jars" in a more distinctive style aroused great interest among spectators. Short sketches and novels from the Qing Dynasty often contained written descriptions of this act. There is an account of Jar Juggl-er Wang, an acrobat in Tianqiao (the Heaven-ly Bridge) in Beijing in the *Qing Bai Lei Chao* (*Collected Short Sketches of the Qing Dynas-ty*) written by Xu Ke. He writes that in the first lunar month of the year 1900, during the Guangxu reign, in a theatre in the captial, a performer named Wang displayed his art of juggling jars as if they were as light as bal-loons. Hence, he became known as Jar Jug-gler Wang. Xu Ke writes, "At first he threw and caught the jar with both hands, revolv-ing it on his arms, shoulders and back. Then he stood as if riding astride a horse and threw the jar underneath his legs, letting it glide over his back and leap over his head.

Then he caught it with his forehead with a load noise. People worried for his head, but he remained complacent. The jar stood on his forehead without being supported by his hands. He nodded repeatedly while the jar spinned on his forehead, upright or up-side down, vertically or horizontally. . . . After a short while, he nodded energetically and the jar flew up, hitting the beam of the room. He let it fall to the ground, which was shaken by the motion, but the jar suffer-ed no damage. He again juggled the jar in the same way as before . . . manoeuvring it with one arm and revolving it around the arm just like a windmill. Spectators saw the jar without seeing the arm. Next he ma-noeuvred it with both arms, revolving it both on the left and right sides. People seemed to see two jars, each revolving around one arm, the two not colliding with each other. As a matter of fact, there was only one jar."

Xu Ke goes on to tell how Jar Juggler Wang threw the jar aloft several times and caught it with his back, waist, hip, knees and feet. This vivid description dramatically depicted Jar Juggler Wang's superb skills.

New Achievements in "Vocal Mimicry"

"Vocal Mimicry" underwent a long pro-cess of development for more than 2,000 years. It became a most popular stage per-formance in the Ming and Qing dynasties. There were two types of mimicry, "Vocal Mimicry" imitating the chirping of birds and other sounds and "Adjoining Shows" which imitated the sounds of selected scenes from daily life. An "Adjoining Show" usually mimicked trifles in the life of townspeople, such as "Five Boys Upset the Study", "Fami-ly Reunion", "A Drunkard Returns Home" and "A Quarrel Between a Husband and Wife". An artist usually performed behind a screen. Artists of "Vocal Mimicry" have perfected and handed down many selected scenes of fascinating "Adjoining Shows". "Fire Fighting", a selected scene, has been the one most praised. Experts call this se-lected scene "a show with strongest appeal". An early account of this performance was found in a short sketch written by an author from the Ming Dynasty. The following is the description of a presentation by one performer in the capital who was known for his superb skills at "Vocal Mimicry."

"One day, many guests attended a grand banquet in the northeastern corner of a hall. An three-metre-wide folding screen was placed there and the performer of 'Vocal Mimicry' sat inside the screen, with only a table, a chair, a fan and a ruler. The guests sat around the screen. In a little while, the rapping of the ruler was heard; silence reigned over the hall and no one dared make any noise.... From a distance was heard the explosion of a fire, the howling of wind. All at once hundreds of sounds mingled with hundreds of voices shouting for help. There were the sounds of the crumbling of a house, and the pouring of water. All the sounds which needed to be included were produced. Even if a person had 100 hands and each hand had 100 fingers, they would not be sufficient to make all of the sounds. If a person had 100 mouths and each mouth had 100 tongues, they would not be sufficient to describe the place. All of the guests became panic-stricken and rushed away from their seats. Their legs trembled. They vyed with one another to leave the place first. Then suddenly the ruler was rapped, and all of the sounds vanished in an instant. When the screen was removed, there were only a man, a table, a fan and a ruler."

Liao Zhai Zhi Yi (*Strange Tales of Liaozhai*) written by Pu Songling (1640-1715), a famous writer of the Qing Dynasty, contains an even more vivid account of an "Adjoining Show" entitled "Vocal Impersonation", as follows:

"A young woman, aged 24 or 25, came to a village, carrying a medical bag. She dispensed medical treatment to earn her livelihood. When patients came to ask for treatment, she would not prescribe medicine for them. She waited until night to ask for advice from the gods.

"In the evening she cleaned a small room and shut herself up in it. Patients would stand around the door and windows and listen quietly. They did not even dare to cough. All was quiet inside and out. When it was almost midnight, the sound of a door curtain lifting was heard. The voice of the practitioner said from inside: 'Has Ninth Cousin come?' A woman's voice replied 'Yes, she has come.' The young practitioner asked again: 'Has Wintersweet come with Ninth Cousin?' A girl seeming to be a maid answered: 'Yes, she has come too.' The three women seemed to chatter on and on. A short while later, the sound of the door curtain rings was heard again. The young practitioner said: 'Sixth Cousin has come.' Another woman said: 'Has Spring Plum Blossom also come 'carrying her baby boy?' A woman said: 'Such a naughty boy! I just could not get him to sleep. He was determined to come with me. He is so heavy to carry. I am dead tired!' Then came the sound of the practitioner solicitously asking the guests to take seats, the sound of Ninth Cousin's inquiry about health, Sixth Cousin's greetings, two maids greeting each other and the child laughing with joy. A hubbub of voices!

"In a moment the woman was heard speaking with a laugh: 'The litttle baby-boy must really be fond of his pet, carrying a cat over such a great distance.' Then the sounds faded away. Again the sound of lifting a door curtain. Everybody in the room spoke at once. Someone said: 'Why does Fourth Cousin come so late?' A young girl replied in a gentle voice: 'The journey is nearly 500 kilometres. I've walked with Auntie for so many hours and have only got here. Auntie has walked at such a slow pace.'

"Then each of them extended greetings, talking about the weather. The sounds of shifting seats and telling a maid to bring more seats, one sound rising after another. The room was permeated with diverse noises. It became quiet only after the time of a meal.

"Immediately the practitioner was heard inquiring about the treatment of the cases. Ninth Cousin thought it good to prescribe ginseng, Sixth Cousin suggested the root of milk vetch while Fourth Cousin advised a spleen-strengthening medicinal herb. They consulted among themselves for a while. Then Ninth Cousin was heard calling for writing brushes and an inkstone. In a minute a series of sounds were heard: ripping and folding paper, clattering of the copper sheath of the writing brush when thrown on the table, the sound of grinding the inkstone against the slab, the rattling of the writing brush on the table top and the stacking and packing of the medicinal herbs in a parcel. Again after a short while, the practitioner came out of the room, called the names of the patients and gave them the prescriptions and medicine before returning to the room. Then the three cousins were heard saying goodbye and also the three maids. Again the babble of the baby boy and the mewing of the cat were heard at the same time. The voice of Ninth Cousin was clear and stirring, that of Sixth Cousin slow but vigorous and that of Fourth Cousin delicate and sweet. And the voices of the three maids, each with its distinctive tone. The listeners could distinguish the different voices. The patients were all astonished, thinking the performance miraculous, but when they tried the medicines they did not find them so effective. Through vocal impersonation, the practitioner advertised her healing art."

This obviously was a story fabricated by the author, but it does reflect the skills of "Vocal Mimicry" of the Qing Dynasty performers.

"Adjoining Shows" gradually fell into oblivion in the late 18th century and they have now vanished. But many famous masters have appeared from among performers of "vocal mimicry" to present their skills to the public.

An expert of "Vocal Mimicry", named Yang, who was popular during the Qing Dynasty, mimicked the chirping of birds and the sounds of insects in an absolutely lifelike fashion. In particular, he excelled in the singing of the song-thrush. He was able to reproduce the sounds with many variations, sometimes seeming to be distant, sometimes near. People called him Song-Thrush Yang. It is said that his voice, when mimicking a parrot's call for tea, had a tinge of delicate timidness as if a young girl were peeping at a window. When he mimicked a pair of phoenixes cooing to each other, it sounded as if the twang of a lute floated in the sky, sometimes clear, sometimes indistinct, showing his accurate voice control. His mimicry of a cock crowing at midnight, the chirping of a cricket in a desolate place outside a town, an oriole or a lark, all made the listeners feel as if they were on the scene. His vocal mimicry often aroused nostalgic emotions, and a listener could even be moved to tears.

The performances of "Hundred-Birds" Zhang, an expert of vocal mimicry during the late Qing Dynasty, were also superb. According to records, in May 1890, Xia Xiaoyan and other scholars sojourning in Beijing, held a wine party to discuss literary writings at the Shishahai Lake in the northern part of the city. Many birds gathered there in the woods, and the scholars felt pleasant and refreshed. At this moment "Hundred-Birds" Zhang came to the party to demonstrate his skills. Standing outside a window, he mimicked the chirping of birds; male or female, large or small, distant or near, at high or low pitch, and all were very stirring. He held a dialogue with birds in the woods. Finally he exhibited his marvellous skill by inspiring all the birds in the woods to chirp in unison.

Acrobatics and Magic in Classical Drama

The drama, began to flourish during the Yuan Dynasty (1271-1368) and gradually developed into an integrated stage art. Acrobatic skills were widely used in drama during the Ming and Qing dynasties. This may be attributed to three factors: One, both can be traced to the same origin. At one time there was no definite division between acrobatics and drama, and so acrobatic skills continued to be present in drama. Two, in the drama of the early stage there were a number of theatrical items in which acrobatic skills were the main content. Three, many roaming acrobats served as performers of stunts in plays.

During the early Ming Dynasty, in the 14th century, acrobatics and other theatrical forms were often performed on the stage at the same time. The circumstances somewhat changed during the middle of the Ming Dynasty. At that time classical drama and acrobatics had a more clear-cut division of work. Sometimes, to better interpret the plot and improve the effects of a performance, many demonstrations of acrobatic skills were added to the scenes including ghosts and spirits in hell in the operas on the theme of Mulian (one of Sakyamuni's 10 disciples). Zhang Dai, a man of letters who lived between the Ming and the Qing dynasties, in his book *Tao An Meng Yi* (*Reminiscences in Taoan Studio*), describes the display of acrobatic skills in the opera "Mulian Rescues His Mother":

It was the practice that prior to the performance of this opera, a large stage was put up on a military drill ground and 30 to 40 performers good at acrobatic fighting were chosen from among opera actors in an Anhui opera troupe. In general, an opera on the theme of Mulian would go on for three days and three nights. First, the acrobatic acts of Rope Walking, Feats on a Table, Feats on a Ladder, Turning Somersaults, Handstands, Juggling Jars and Stone Mortars, Rope Twirling, Jumping Through a Fire Gateway, and so forth, were performed. Immediately afterwards, were scenes in hell, and characters appeared such as the deities of heaven and earth, ghostly guards of the nether regions, goddesses of hell, Ghosts of Misfortune, hell runners and demons. All sorts of instruments of torture such as saws, grindstones, cauldrons, huge cooking pots, a mountain of swords, blocks of ice and trees of broadswords were used.

When the show was presented, to act out the arrest of monk Mulian's mother, the arch-villain, Mulian's mother escaped out of the opera shed and ran around the stage with the ghosts chasing close after her. Meanwhile, they juggled many sharp steel pitchforks, accurately nailing them to the ceilings and beams of the sheds. The pitchforks appeared to be falling down. Mulian's mother dodged and fled, tumbling about again and again. At this time, thousands of spectators in and around the shed shouted in unison. The noise was so thunderous that it created a terrifying atmosphere, and local officials thought pirates had got ashore and were panic-stricken.

An opera on the theme of monk Mulian was similar to an acrobatic show with a plot, and so opera stars required help from performers of other branches of theatrical art. It was necessary for quite a number of acrobats to join in the presentation of such operas. Gu Qiyuan of the Ming Dynasty said that during the Wanli reign (1573-1620), magic acts, feats of back bending and brandishing long flags were often interspersed among the opera performances. All these required the participation of acrobats.

During the Qing Dynasty, the stunts became the highlight of the performances of "Monk Mulian" operas. When Emperor Kang Xi (reigning 1661-1722) watched a "Monk Mulian" opera in 1683, real tigers, elephants and horses performed on stage in addition to various sorts of acrobatics.

In addition to "Monk Mulian" operas there were also selected scenes such as the performance of a "Great Variety of Acrobatic Skills" and "Da Lian Xiang" (a folk show in which the performer sings and dances while juggling a club threaded with bronze coins). The former tells the story of a married couple who had to roam from place to place to eke out a living by means of their performances. Their money was extorted by a local despot. In this performance the use of swinging meteors was interspersed with the acting. The presentation involved martial clowns and martial female roles in the performance of the classical opera. It became the convention to include acrobatic acts in operas on martial subjects. "Parry and Thrust" were most widely used in the operas of modern times. Such parry and thrust movements were executed by juggling weapons with the hands and feet, and juggling weapons between warrior opponents. There were a great variety of tricks, patterns and devices. Later, acrobatic skills were used in operas on civil themes. For instance, "Throwing Up of Cap" and "Juggling of Boots" when expressing the mood of anxiety or anger of a character requires the use of stunts in an opera.

Vicissitudes of a Hundred Years

Folk performers in the Ming and Qing dynasties achieved new successes in acrobatic art. But they lived under very harsh conditions, especially the small itinerant acrobatic groups, that were composed mostly of folk performers.

Yu Chu Xin Zhi (*A New Collection of Yuchu*), a 20-volume collection of articles compiled by Zhang Chao of the Qing Dynasty, contained short pieces by writers from the late Ming and early Qing dynasties. An informal essay entitled "Watching Competitive Contests at Jiuniuba" describes a touring performance of folk acrobats between the Ming and Qing dynasties as follows:

"One day, a small acrobatic group came to Jiuniuba. Elderly peasants of this hilly village sponsored the performance on this occasion. They put up a makeshift thatched stage and fenced in a plot of open-air ground for an arena set up under the trees along a stream. Villagers gathered on the threshing grounds. When the performance began, a woman acrobat lay on a table, juggling a six-year-old boy who performed the movements of 'A Boy Making Obeisance to the Goddess of Mercy' and 'Lotus Flower Coming Out of Water'. Two men, and two women stood by the side of the table, beating gongs and drums and singing folk songs to the rhythm of the movements. Immediately afterward, another woman performed 'Juggling a Table' and 'Juggling a Wooden Mallet' with her feet. A man performed 'Juggling a Ladder', also with his feet. After the performance, the elderly villagers offered them food and drinks. They then moved to a slope and went on with their performance. The man walked on 2.5-metre-high stilts, singing while fanning himself and then brandished a heavy halberd. The last act was 'Rope Walking'. The rope, about 10 metres long, was suspended three metres above the ground. A woman performer displayed gymnastic skills on it while lying on her back. She also performed 'A Cockerel Standing on One Foot', and 'Carrying a Load on a Shoulder Pole', as well as being suspended from the rope, jumping through hoops and rope walking while blindfolded. Throughout the performance there was the beating of gongs and drums and singing to the rhythm of the movements.

"Through their inquiry the villagers knew that the performers came from Henan. Owing to the heavy taxes in their home village, they could not keep body and soul together. So the acrobat had to roam with his wife and infant, his wife's sister-in-law and the son of his brother to earn a livelihood here and there. They had been performing for three generations. If they had any surplus from their income as strolling performers, they brought it back to the home village to pay taxes. This small group toured Jiangsu, Zhejiang, Guangdong, Guangxi, Yunnan and Guizhou. Traversing long distance, crossing mountains and rivers, they always walked on foot while carrying shoulder poles. They regarded roads as their home and perform-

ance as their farmland. Both boys and girls began to learn acrobatic art at the age of five or six so they could have something to live on when they were older. They were in rags and showed the fatigue of long journeys but they knew how to enjoy life, and lived in harmony as a close-knit group."

This was an accurate picture of the organizational form and miserable life of Chinese strolling performers who were engaged in horsemanship and acrobatics. In the several centuries from the Ming and Qing dynasties to the eve of Liberation, such family-type itinerant acrobatic groups could be seen across China. Especially after the Opium War in 1840, rural economy declined with each passing day. Many poor peasants who had acrobatic skills had to leave their home villages and became "performers of horsemanship and acrobatics" (Figure 66).

In the 100 years between the Opium War and the founding of New China, traditional Chinese acrobatics met unprecedented misfortune. In the semi-feudal and semi-colonial society, under the oppression of imperialism, feudalism and bureaucrat-capitalism,

66. Painting of a roadside acrobatic performer by an anonymous painter from the Qing Dynasty

67. "Climbing a Mountain of Knives"
— Woodcut from the Qing Dynasty.

the Chinese people were disaster-ridden. Folk acrobatics which had been degraded to the lowest rung of society suffered most. Its performers had a very insignificant social status. They were brutally exploited and unable to make ends meet. Quite a number of performers had to change their profession and work as coolies or peddlers. Many fine traditional items were gradually lost. Some performers went abroad and stayed there until they died. To earn a livelihood, some performers had to present vulgar acts to cater to spectators seeking sensuous stimulus. Consequently, acrobatic art lost its rustic simplicity. Its development was tainted by feudalism and colonialism.

Tricks of torture appeared, such as "Swal-lowing a Knife", "Spitting Fire" and "Dismantling a Human Body into Eight Pieces". There also appeared, during the late Qing Dynasty, tricks such as, "Climbing a Mountain of Knives" (Figure 67) and other acts of cruelty and horror.

Even in the 20th century, whenever amusement parks found their business languish, they put up playbills advertizing "Dancing on Broken Pieces of Glass", "Rolling Over a Board with Nails", "Swallowing Five Poisonous Creatures" (scorpion, viper, centipede, house lizard and toad) and similar items to attract the theatre-goers. These acrobatic numbers were not only harmful to the physical and mental health of the performers, they were also lacking in artistic value. During such acts the performers sustained extremely great suffering at the risk of their lives, and it was called "scooping up food from a basin of blood". At that time "strolling performers" often did an act of "Suspending Oneself by a Queue" in front of a tea house or a theatre. With his hair braided, the performer suspended himself by his queue in mid-air, without any support for his limbs. He would swing to and fro or present variety shows in the air. A certain performer, known as "Flying Queue", specialized in doing boxing in the air. Once, during a show, something went wrong with the hook which suspended him. He dropped down and died instantly.

Performers going abroad could not avoid such suffering either. The bosses of some foreign circus troupes attracted spectators by requiring Chinese performers to present such atrocious items as "Trio Suspension in Mid-air". Huge playbills did everything possible to exaggerate how three Chinese performers could be suspended in mid-air by the queues on their heads while at the same time, chatting, laughing, eating food and drinking wine. As a matter of fact, these performers had to suppress their pain, humiliation and tears in order to earn a livelihood.

At the time of the late Qing Dynasty, folk performers went to Europe, the Americas, Japan and Southeast Asia to introduce traditional Chinese acrobatics and magic to audiences abroad. They went with sons, nephews and apprentices, and carried their animals and simple stage properties.

Zhu Liankui, a magician of Yangliuqing in Tianjin, went abroad in the 1870's. He performed Chinese magic with an American circus troupe. His magic acts, full of oriental flavour, caused a sensation in the United States and Europe. His professional name was "Jinling Fu", and he was well known among magicians abroad.

Han Bingqian was an expert in performing "Traditional-Style Conjuring". He went with his apprentices, sons and nephews on performance tours to 19 countries in Europe and the United States for about 10 years. While presenting traditional Chinese magic acts, they systematically learned Western magic and bought foreign stage properties. After returning to China, Han Bingqian's

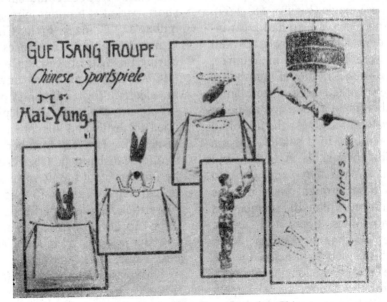

68. Advertisement of performances by Chinese acrobats roaming abroad during the late Qing Dynasty.

69. Photograph of a performance by Chinese acrobats roaming abroad before Liberation.

troupe became a new-style magic troupe. His nephew Han Jingwen, and his apprentices Zhang Jingfu and Zhao Jingxi became famous magicians and comic actors. They produced a deep impact on the development of modern Chinese magic (Figures 68 & 69).

Sun Fuyou and Chen Yubao had great influence on modern Chinese acrobatics and circus. They were both born in Wuqiao, Hebei Province — the home of acrobatics in China. They worked hard at acrobatics from childhood and had a good command of skills in this branch of art. At the age of 10 they went as members of a small acrobatic group to display their skills in Russia and Southeast Asia. When they came back to China, each of them brought back a large circus troupe with more than 100 members as well as elephants, lions, tigers and horses. Moreover, they became versed in aerial acrobatic numbers such as "Feats on the Flying Trapeze" and "Feats on the Trampoline" and "Acrobatic Stunts on a Rope". These acts had not been seen in China before that time.

However, because the Chinese government levied exorbitant taxes and there were frequent wars in those days, people did not have sufficient livelihood. Therefore, the magic and circus troupes could survive for noly a short period. Famous circus expert Chen Yubao's "China's First Circus Troupe" returned to give performances in the country during the War of Resistance Against Japan (1937-1945). As he was unwilling to lend his elephant for the funerary procession of a prominent capitalist, the elephant was poisoned to death and his other animals were dispersed. His 150-member circus troupe had to be disbanded. Chen Yubao and other performers could only give acrobatic acts in amusement parks to eke out a living. Nevertheless, these performers were determined to develop Chinese acrobatic art and sowed the seeds of modern acrobatics, circus, magic, and comic acts.

This was an important 100-year period, when Chinese ancient and traditional acrobatics changed drastically, and modern acrobatics burgeoned. The Opium War forced open the door of China to other countries and there were increasing chances for international intercourse. British, German and Japanese magic and circus troupes came one after the other. Their performances instilled new inspiration into Chinese acrobatics and magic.

Meanwhile, more Chinese acrobats went abroad every year. While spreading Chinese acrobatic skills among other countries, they learned quite a number of things from their counterparts in Europe, the United States and Japan. They began to assimilate foreign ways of management, formed new troupes and performed new acts.

In particular, after the anti-imperialist and anti-feudal May 4th Movement of 1919, under the influence of the new cultural movement, a number of intellectuals also plunged themselves into the study and work of acrobatics and magic. All these factors promoted the reform of age-old traditional Chinese acrobatics and laid a good foundation for the formation and development of modern acrobatics.

7. Modern Acrobatics in Full Bloom

Du Fu, renowned Chinese poet of the Tang Dynasty, wrote two lines of poetry full of philosophical significance:

Day after day time and human events urge each other on,

Spring begins its return at the Winter Solstice.

In the early 1950's, with the founding of New China, acrobatic art which had withered after going through wretched circumstances ushered in its spring at long last. Traditional culture of the Chinese nation has won unprecedented esteem under the socialist system. Acrobatics, which had formerly been degraded to the lowest rung of the social ladder, has emerged like a sparkling gem out of the earth. In the last 32 years, on the basis of inheriting and carrying forward national and folk traditions, acrobatics has absorbed and blended some elements of other performing arts, while at the same time borrowing from foreign experience. Thus, modern Chinese acrobatics has gradually come into being, embodying the spirit of our times and possessing a unique national style.

A Mighty Contingent of Acrobats

After the founding of New China, reconstruction took place, and previously neglected tasks were undertaken. In 1950, shortly after the First National Congress of Writers and Artists, the Ministry of Culture of the Central People's Government set about establishing an acrobatic troupe to prepare organizationally for the revival of the traditional acrobatic arts. The late Premier Zhou Enlai summoned competent functionaries on art work and administration to engage in preparations for this task. He personally attended to the selection of the acrobatic acts as well as to the ideological style, previous artistic training and living conditions of the performers.

In October 1950 outstanding acrobats from Shanghai, Tianjin, Beijing, Wuhan and Shenyang presented a performance in the Huairen Hall in Zhongnanhai, Beijing — the political centre of New China. Each demonstrated his or her own masterpiece. The performance included Guan Yuhe's "Jumping Through Hoops," He Shuwang's "Jar Tricks", "Cycling" by Jin Yeqin and his younger sister, Yang Xiaoting's "Traditional-Style Conjuring", "Juggling with the Hands" by Chen Laben and his younger brother, the "Diabolo Play" by Wang Guiying and her younger sister, the "Pagoda of Bowls" by Cheng Shaolin and his younger brother, Yin Yuhong's "Spinning Plates" and the "Feats on the Bar" by Cao Pengfei and his younger brother. Pooling their efforts, the acrobats also gave a group performance of "The Pyramid" (Figure 70). This was the first acrobatic performance in New China and also the first step Chinese acrobatic arts had taken in weeding through the old to bring forth the new. The items presented were wholesome, possessing simplicity and grace, and richly tinged with national characteristics. They reflected the Chinese people's new mental outlook.

The late Chairman Mao Zedong, Chairman Liu Shaoqi, Premier Zhou Enlai, Chairman of the Standing Committee of the National People's Congress, Zhu De, and other party and government leaders attended this performance and gave it high praise and encouragement. They decided that these acrobats should form a troupe as a cultural delegation of New China to tour European countries. Thus New China's first acrobatic troupe came into being. At that time Premier Zhou Enlai named it Zhonghua (China) Acrobatic Troupe — the predecessor of the China Acrobatic Troupe of Beijing (Figure 71).

The news of the birth of this acrobatic troupe, and its visit to other countries, warmed the hearts of thousands of acrobats who were scattered in different places. They rejoiced and hastened to tell the news to one another. Many acrobats roaming abroad returned to the motherland and were willing to contribute to the revival of traditional acrobatic arts and to serving the people with their professional skills. As a result, acrobatic troupes, magic troupes and circus troupes were set up in quick succession in different parts of the country.

70. Group performance of "The Pyramid" by the first acrobatic troupe of New China.

71. Test of professional skills at the first enrolment of performers for the first acrobatic troupe of New China.

Corps Acrobatic Troupe, as well as the Railway Acrobatic Troupe, catering mainly to the railway workers. There were also privately owned professional troupes formed by the acrobats, for example, the Zhang Huichong Magic Troupe headed by magician Zhang Huichong and the Red Acrobatic Troupe headed by acrobat Pan Yushan.

The establishment of acrobatic troupes was a means of reorganizing and remoulding the then existing ranks of acrobats. Most acrobatic groups which survived from the old society retained some of the aspects of feudalism. Some bosses of acrobatic troupes were actually representatives of cruel exploitation who had close connections with the dark forces of society. In the course of establishing the acrobatic troupes throughout the country, it was possible to eliminate a small number of local ruffians and hooligans, feudal gangbosses and parasites — dregs of the old society. A small number of persons considered not suitable for the field of acrobatics were given other employment. Some acrobats with unique skills, who had had to find other jobs to earn their livelihood, were persuaded to return to the profession of acrobatics. A number of dancers, musicians and artists, engaged in creative literature and art, were sent to replenish the ranks of acrobatic artists. These new-style writers and artists cooperated closely with acrobats and infused fresh blood into the acrobatic arts. Consequently acrobatics made great progress both in the composition and in the coordination of music, dance and stage art. This enhanced the artistry of acrobatic performances.

New-style acrobatic troupes contributed to the development of modern Chinese acrobatics. Particularly noted were the earliest troupes established in the 1950's such as the China Acrobatic Troupe, the Shanghai Acrobatic Troupe, the Wuhan Acrobatic Troupe, the Chongqing Acrobatic Troupe

They numbered more than 200 professional acrobatic troupes in a few years. Among them were state-owned organizations set up by provinces, municipalities or autonomous regions, as well as army acrobatic troupes. Those formed by the ministries and commissions of the central government for their special requirements included the Fighters' Acrobatic Troupe, serving mainly the People's Liberation Army, and the Railway and the Shenyang Acrobatic Troupe as well as the Advance Acrobatic Troupe and the Fighters' Acrobatic Troupe of the army. They have been the largest troupes in New China, producing the most far-reaching influence. They have done a great deal of work and have provided a very good precedent in weeding through the old to bring forth the new, and in training acrobats to serve the people and to become a bridge in promoting friendship between the people of China and other countries in the world.

During the "cultural revolution" (1966-1976) the Gang of Four, represented by Jiang Qing, unscrupulously exercised fascist dictatorship in the realm of literature and art. The ranks of acrobats were seriously damaged, being reduced by nearly a half. And not until 1972, when Premier Zhou Enlai attended to the questions in the field of acrobatics, did acrobatic troupes begin to resume their work. According to initial statistics there are now 124 professional acrobatic troupes with more than 12,000 members. These include those from the county level upwards in different parts of the country, in the army, and in various industries.

The acrobatic troupes in the provinces, municipalities and autonomous regions first serve the people in their own regions. They also go on tours so that audiences throughout the country have the opportunity to appreciate acrobatic performances of different styles and with different special features. Divided into a number of groups, bringing their own costumes and stage props, and sometimes crossing mountains and rivers, they go to factories, villages, army units, sea ports, forests, remote areas and frontier outposts to perform for the builders and defenders of New China. In the past three decades this mighty contingent of acrobats have travelled all over China. This spirit of working hard and warmheartedly serving the people has been highly praised and many acrobatic troupes have been commended as advanced collectives. (Figure 72).

Beginning with the China Acrobatic Troupe, the first one in New China to make a

72. Acrobatic troupes give performances in factories and villages.

performance tour abroad, more than 30 acrobatic troupes have gone abroad on some 100 occasions to give excellent shows to audiences in more than 100 countries on five continents. This has promoted mutual understanding and deep friendship between the peoples of China and other countries and has made new contributions to Chinese and foreign cultural exchange. Chinese acrobats have also trained many acrobatic performers for friendly countries such as Tanzania, Egypt, Sudan and Ghana and consequently have spread China's age-old acrobatic arts (Figures 73a-f).

In addition to professional troupes, China also has numerous amateur acrobats. Acrobatics as a hobby has a long tradition.

73 a   The China Acrobatic Troupe greets the audience at the end of a performance in London.

73 b   Performers chat with British friends during the intermission of a performance of the China Acrobatic troupe.

73 c   During a performance of the China Acrobatic Troupe in Stockholm, a performer goes off stage and fishes up a living fish in the midst of the audience.

73 d. Sudanese acrobatic trainee practises walking on a steel wire under the guidance of a Chinese coach

73 f. Egyptian performers trained by the China Acrobatic Troupe

Many factories, mines, rural areas, army units and schools have their own amateur acrobatic and magic groups. These amateur acrobats practise skills and make stage props in their spare time. At festivals and on holidays they perform in parks, clubs or in the fields to enliven the cultural life of the people. Some amateur groups have consistantly given performances for 20 to 30 years, with some superb masters emerging out of them.

Wuqiao County in Hebei Province, Liaocheng Prefecture in Shandong Province, Yan-

73 e. Sudanese acrobatic trainees practise cycling

cheng in Jiangsu Province and Tianmen in Hubei Province are known for the origin of some forms of acrobatics in China. Amateur acrobatic activities are widespread in these places. Almost every household has acrobatic, magic and circus talents; and some families boast of their own unique acrobatic skills carried through several generations. This mighty army of amateur acrobats has supplied a continuous stream of talented performers to professional troupes (Figures 74 & 75).

The First Congress of Chinese Acrobats was held in Beijing between October 28 and November 3, 1981. More than 170 delegates from different parts of China gathered together to sum up and exchange experiences and to discuss plans for further development. The Association of Chinese Acrobats was established at this congress — an unprecedented and great event in the history of Chinese acrobatics. Famous acrobat Xia Juhua was elected chairman of the association. As a national people's organization, the association is determined to unite everybody in the field of acrobatic arts, steadily promote its development, strengthen its research work and raise modern Chinese acrobatics to new heights (Figure 76).

74. An old peasant in Wuqiao, Hebei Province, teaches his grandchildren to practise handstands.

75. An amateur acrobatic performance by peasants of Anhui Province.

76. The founding of the Association of Chinese Acrobats in Beijing.

Bringing Forth the New Out of the Old

"Let a hundred flowers blossom and weed through the old to bring forth the new" and "make the past serve the present and foreign things serve China" are the policies for literature and the arts as set forth by the Party Central Committee at the founding of New China. Guided by these principles, profound changes have been brought about in the age-old art of acrobatics.

Chinese acrobatic arts have been marked by vicissitudes for over 2,000 years, gradually changing from court entertainments into itinerant shows. This protracted and tortuous evolution left many remnants from the old society. A lot of feudal superstition, vulgarity, cruelty and horror have been mixed into an abundantly artistic acrobatic heritage. How to assimilate the essence of the artistry and reject the feudal remnants is an arduous task for the acrobats of New China. Beginning with the founding of the first acrobatic troupe, acrobats have given primary importance to the work of "weeding through the old to bring forth the new".

In the early 1950's, Premier Zhou Enlai said: "Acrobatics should give people an aesthetic appreciation and a pleasant sensation. Neither deformity nor excessive stimulus should be used to attract the audience." Premier Zhou Enlai's instruction has become the motto for the acrobats. Retaining what is the quintessence and discarding the dross, they took the first step to improve acrobatics — banning those presentations harmful to the mental and physical health of the performers and those which unduly stimulated the senses of the spectators. Some of the presentations banned were, "Climbing a Mountain of Knives", "Dismantling a Human Body into Eight Pieces", "Swallowing a Sword", "Rolling on a Board Studded with Nails", "Eating an Electric Bulb", "Dancing on Broken Pieces of Glass", "Swallowing Five Poisonous Creatures" (scorpion, viper, centipede, house lizard and toad) and "A Snake Worms into Eyes, Ears, Nostrils and Mouth". Meanwhile, efforts were made to study and improve upon a number of fine traditional presentations such as "Diabolo Play", "Jumping Through Hoops on the Ground", "Conjuring Tricks", "Handstands on a Pyramid of Chairs", "Cycling", "Jar Tricks" and "Juggling with the Hands". These wholesome, lively items with artistic execution, which reflected national characteristics, were refreshing to the audience.

In the old acrobatic arena, acts were performed such as "All-Purpose Feet" and "Dwarf's Comic Acts" which made use of a person's physiological defects to attract more spectators. Some unfortunate persons who were dwarfs or who had congenital malformations became victims for the bosses of acrobatic troupes who sought profit. There was a person who was born without upper limbs and had to use his feet in stead of his hands to handle everyday activities. His feet had become very skillful having used them from the time of his childhood. A certain capitalist hit upon this as a good way for his troupe to make money. He asked this deformed person to perform, with naked feet, the movements of kicking apart a wooden tub and piecing together the broken fragments and binding them together with an iron hoop, as an acrobatic act on the stage. He called the act "All-Purpose Feet." Such a performance had neither art nor gymnastic skills worthy of mention. It merely displayed the congenital defect of a deformed person and insulted his personality. Now, the daughter of this handicapped man, actress Quan

Lianti of the Chongqing Acrobatic Troupe, performs a genuine "All-Purpose Feet". She is a distinguished acrobat of "Juggling Light Properties with the Feet" trained in New China. "Juggling Boards with the Feet," "Juggling Cylindrical Tubes with the Feet" and "Juggling Parasols with the Feet", performed by her, are lithe, graceful and highly appreciated by audiences at home and abroad. Her "Whirling a Parasol with One Foot" looks like a lotus leaf rippled by the breeze. This is a far cry from the impaired image of her father who was insulted in former years.

"Rejecting the dross" does not mean only banning a number of acrobatic acts. Sometimes one act may contain both essence and dross. This makes it necessary to study the presentations, one by one, sifting out those vulgar acts, unrelated to acrobatic skills, which strive only to be sensational and breathtaking, and instead of concentrating the performer's efforts on perfecting his artistic skills. For example, "Jar Tricks" is a genuine traditional item and its gymnastic skills lie in the performer's juggling and catching ability, and the use of his hands, feet and head. Historical records contain enchanting accounts of this act. Never-

theless, it was distorted beyond recognition by the time of China's liberation in 1949. To cater to the vulgar taste of a number of spectators, some performers would hum a popular melody and do some funny movements while balancing a heavy jar on their head. Consequently, the art of "Jar Tricks" declined. The famous performer of "Jar Tricks", He Shuwang, as well as other contemporary acrobats have improved upon this item. They recovered its fine tradition of juggling skills, sifted out the portions unrelated to acrobatic skills, and developed numerous techniques of balancing jars and juggling and catching them with their fists, fingers or feet. They also devised a series of new skills with two performers juggling jars to each other, thus making this act more fascinating (Figure 77).

Performances in mid-air no longer just strive to be breathtaking without regard to the performer's safety. Effective protective measures have been taken. All acrobatic troupes are now using safety ropes or nets, and inspecting and repairing stage props regularly. As a result, the performers do not have to worry about their safety and the audience can appreciate the acrobatic skills at ease. Effective safety facilities ensure the perform-

77. He Shuwang's performance of "Jar Tricks".

ers' giving full play to their skills and this encourages the perfection of difficult gymnastic techniques.

In weeding through the old to bring forth the new, acrobats have also paid attention to another important aspect. They no longer, as in the past century, pay attention only to "juggling", "conjuring" and "practising" and neglect the beauty of imagery. The reform aims at turning acrobatics into a visual art, stressing gymnastic skills, while catering to the spectator's aesthetic appreciation as well. So, apart from improving skills, acrobatics must resort to the multiple coordination of costumes, stage properties, lighting, stage design, musical accompaniment and design. Formerly, this was beyond the means of poor strolling acrobats and even the acrobatic stages in regular amusement houses found it hard to afford such facilities. At that time, so long as lamps could serve the purpose of lighting, and costumes and stage properties were passable and coupled with some musical accompaniment, an acrobatic act was regarded as fairly good. Attention could not be paid to whether the images on the stage were graceful or the artistic style was coherent.

To end such backwardness, many acrobatic troupes have gradually established art committees and choreography and directing groups, responsible for the designing of acrobatic arts. Expert acrobats, art directors and coaches, as well as personnel for costume, music and stage design, have drawn up schemes for reform and are attempting to carry out the plans in every aspect. Every act is no longer laden with only difficult skills, but rather represents an integral composition of careful artistic design. As a result, the whole presentation is a combination of rhythm and beautiful images, both coherent and varied. It features the difficulty of gymnastic skills but does not look rigid and dull. The sequence of the performers' acrobatic movements and dance tableaux is arranged

with meticulous care. Costumes, stage properties, stage design, lighting and melodies for musical accompaniment are designed in accordance with the style and characteristics of each presentation, striving to be colourful, attractive, and with a distinctive national style. Hence the performance becomes an artistic entity, harmonious in multiple aspects when presented in front of the audience. An example of this is the "Lion Dance", a traditional acrobatic act coming from the common people, which possesses rich local colour. It stands out in different styles — the elegant southern style and the unrestrained northern style. So, the melodies for musical accompaniment designed for presentation by the Nanjing Acrobatic Troupe is lively and refreshing, while those designed by the Shandong Acrobatic Troupe are passionate and sonorous.

Establishing a system of choreography and art directing was a pioneering act in the field of Chinese acrobatics after Liberation in 1949. All-round artistic refining has enhanced the charm of acrobatic performances. Take "Diabolo Play" for instance. There is a great difference between its presentation in the past and in the present. Diabolo was originally a children's toy seen everywhere. Two wooden sticks each about 0.3-0.4 metre long were joined to the two ends of a string 1-1.3 metres long. A child held the short sticks and wound the string on the axle in the mid-section of the diabolo. The child would spin the diabolo on the string and as it whirled up and down the string, it hummed, the intensity of the sound increasing with the speed. Making use of the diverse ways of string winding, acrobats can display a great variety of patterns in diabolo play. It is an acrobatic act with distinctive national characteristics. But, in the past, an acrobat only practised a few difficult movements and failed to achieve a remarkable effect in performances. In recent years, through steady artistic refining, the item has become more and more fascinating and rich in national flavour, holding spectators spell-bound with appreciation. It has been highly praised by audiences at home and abroad.

Many acrobatic troupes have the presentation of "Diabolo Play" in their repertories. But, with different handling by various choreographers and directors, each performance has its own merits, thus making its artistic form more varied and colourful. In accordance with the customs of the Chinese people, diabolo play is the favourite pastime among girls in their early teens around the Spring Festival (the lunar New Year). So the stage designers of the Chinese Acrobatic Troupe of Beijing dressed the girl acrobats in their holiday best and pinned pink plum blossoms on their black long braids. When these charming maidens appeared on the stage, they imbued people with a sense of joy. The soft lighting and the settings of the blue sky, white snow, plum blossoms and colourful gauze lanterns presented the festive atmosphere of the traditional holidays. Cheerful melodies blended with the humming of the diabolos. The lithe dance steps were harmonious with the whirling diabolos. The audience praised the item as "a symphonic poem full of youthful vitality".

The "Diabolo Play" of the Shanghai Acrobatic Troupe has been mainly performed by veteran artist, Tian Shuangliang. The four female performers only serve to set off his sturdy, vigorous performance. He uses a large brass lid similar to the lid of a teapot, as his stage prop, instead of the diabolo. "Large-Lid Play" is his unique creation. Purplish red velvet curtains set off the large, sparkling golden lid which, whirling up and down, looks like a shooting meteor or a bright moon.

On the other hand, the "Diabolo Play" of the Guangdong Acrobatic Troupe is closely linked with ballet dancing from beginning to end. Bringing into prominence the special feature of a children's pastime, it is enchanting in its own fashion (Colour plate 20).

Strenuous efforts have been made to blend art and technique in the presentation of acrobatics as a performing art. As acrobatics involves special gymnastic agility, it has many limitations. Needless to say, to add a new movement or to change a pattern requires practising for months and even years. Sometimes, the change of a costume, a pair of shoes, a stage property or a light source will affect the performer's being able to give full play to his or her acrobatic skills. Even a slight artistic change in acrobatics cannot be achieved within a short period. Only through the repeated endeavours of two or three generations of acrobats can some items be changed to conform to the criterion of artistic beauty. Consequently the trainees must, from the very beginning, understand the artistic conception in the design of related items. While training them in skills, efforts should be made to enrich their knowledge of music, dance, drama and the fine arts, so as to create the conditions for presenting more beautiful images on the acrobatic stage. In spite of the difficulties, and with the acrobats' persistent efforts, modern Chinese acrobatics has now advanced far ahead of the first programme of acrobatics performed in the Huairen Hall in Zhongnanhai, Beijing, during the early days of New China.

Let a Hundred Flowers Blossom

Thanks to the acrobats' enthusiasm for artistic creation, acrobatic acts have rapidly grown in number and improved in quality. In early post-liberation days acrobatic troupes throughout the country had only a few dozen popular acts. In the 1960's, according to rough estimates, acrobatic acts on the stage increased to nearly 200 and in the 1980's, more new items have appeared. Circus shows and acts with tamed animals, difficult acrobatic skills in mid-air, magic tricks and comic acts have developed to varying extents. Over the past 32 years many good items, which retain our fine national traditions and represent the spirit of our era, have gradually developed into a unique style of acrobatic art in New China.

New life situations provide abundant materials for innovation in acrobatics. The bicycle is people's most commonly used means of transportation in China's cities and countryside. "Cycling", which uses bicycles as stage property, has been developed from a single act into a dozen new acts differing in content and form. The Railway Acrobatic Troupe mainly caters to railway workers and staff, so its members have focussed on "Cycling" which is linked to transportation. They have created a number of new and original acts, including "Group Cycling", "Cycling Tricks","Comic Cycling"and "Unicycling". The programme begins in an unconventional fashion. First, all cycling performers present a dance tableau as soon as they ascend the stage. Then a "Train" drives past at lightning speed, accompanied by a rhythmic melody, played at a fast pace, a bicycle with several acrobats on it serving as the "locomotive" races ahead, guided by a red flag. The "carriages of the train" are composed of a dozen performers riding unicycles one after another, with each putting his hands on the shoulders of the preceding performer to form a procession. With the sounding of a whistle, the "train" travels across the stage in high spirits, conveying to the audience the image of a modern train rolling ahead. Then each performer presents a cycling item. Their "Group Unicycling" is an unusual, exuberant folk dance.

Throughout the presentation the performers on the unicycles interweave different skills of riding such a cycle to a dance rhythm and the fluttering of red silks. Thus they put on a series of new cycling feats brimming with rhythmic beauty (Figure 78).

The Shanghai Post-Telecommunications Cycling Team is an amateur acrobatic organization composed mainly of postmen. Their "Group Cycling" represents a special style. Making use of proficient skills, the performers present a number of pictures, sometimes resembling a large basket laden with fresh flowers, sometime looking like a peacock displaying its fine feathers. The beautiful decorative patterns convey the warm love for life and work cherished by the postal workers who ride bicycles to deliver letters every day. In Chinese folk legends, the peacocks' display of fine feathers symbolizes good luck and prosperity. This technique shown on a bicycle, and initiated by the Post-Telecommunications Cycling Team, has been warmly received by audiances. Many professional acrobatic troupes have striven hard to learn this group tableau on a bicycle. At first, the "Peacock Displaying Its Fine Feathers" was put on by seven to eight male performers. It is now performed by an all-women cast of 14. It is, indeed, beyond praise that the performer serving as the base on the bicycle carries the huge 500-kilogramme-heavy "peacock" to "soar" with effortless ease (Colour plate 21).

The "Duet Cycling" by Liu Zhangshu and his wife, "Cycling Feats in a Continuous Stream" by Zhao Yanping and his younger sister Zhao Yanyan, as well as "Comic Cycling" by Jin Yeqin, all display special cycling skills. Ten to 20 cycling movements form an organic whole, without interval; nor does the bicycle ever come to a halt. With nimble movements and variations at marvellous speed, all these acts on the bycycles have their own unique styles (Colour plate 22). In addition, "Kicking and Balancing Bowls on

78. "The Train of Our Era" by the Railway Acrobatic Troupe.

Unicycles", "Feats on Uncycles", "Kicking Properties to Each Other on Two Unicycles" and "A Human Pyramid on a Unicycle" all are new acts which have come into being in recent years (Colour plates 23 & 24).

Another category of cycling consists of displaying acrobatic skills on a stationary bicycle, called "Feats on a Stationary Bicycle". Originally it was only one movement of a cycling performance. Owing to the efforts of two to three generations of acrobats in New China, it has become an important category of cycling. Various acrobatic troupes present "Balancing on a Stationary Bicycle", "Kicking and Balancing a Ladder on a Unicycle" and "Balancing a Pole on a Stationary Bicycle". Only when a bicycle maintains balance in fast movement, does it facilitate performers doing all kinds of superb gymnastic movements. But the performance of "Feats on a Stationary Bicycle" breaks away from this principle. Performers calmly display balancing skills with grace and ease on a bicycle which stands still on a high rack, without support on any side. A performer does diverse calisthenic poses on

the tottering bicycle; sometimes standing on the axle of the back wheel, he lifts up the front part of the bicycle and whirls it 360 degrees. In recent years "Feats on a Stationary Bicycle" have involved a greater variety of movements and more attractive calisthenics, showing the wisdom and extraordinary courage of the new generation of performers (Colour plate 25).

New presentations drawn and refined directly from life are not confined to cycling. They are seen in nearly every major category of acrobatics, for instance, "Children's Swing Board" in aerial items, "Cooks" in comic acts, and "Monkey Tricks" and "Training a Panda" in presentations involving animal taming. "An Outpost at Coastal Defence" and "Early Morning in the Countryside" in vocal mimicry, "Table Tennis Balls Convey Friendship" and "Conjuring Calligraphy and Painting" in magic acts are all successful works (Colour plates 26 & 27).

Quite a number of new acts have evolved out of old ones. For example, "Rope Walking" was an age-old traditional item. The stage property for rope walking consisted

— 110 —

20.   "Diabolo Play".

21.   Group cycling: "Peacock Displaying Its Feathers".

25. "Balancing on a Stationary Bicycle": Three performers one on top of the other while performing handstands, with hands grabbing knees.

26. Comic performance: "Cooks".

27. Comic performance: "Humourous Violinist".

28. "Silk Dance on Steel Wire".

29. "Somersaults on Steel Wire".

30. "Two Performers Kicking Parasols to Each Other".

31. "Jar Juggling" by two performers.

32. "Springboard Stunts and Juggling People".

33. "Balancing Benches on the Feet".

35. "V-Formation Balancing Act on Stacked Chairs" performed by the Guangzhou Children's Acrobatic Group.

34. New shooting technique: "Shooting with the Feet".

36. "Lion Dance".

37. New developments
of handstand techniques.

38. Calisthenics: "Flying Goddesses".

39. "Rolling with
a Cup of Water"
performed by Dai
Wenxia.

40. "Jumping Through
Hoops" — in the style
of a flying swallow.

41. "Balancing Feats on a Swaying Board".

42. "Kicking the Shuttlecock".

45. Magic: "One Ball Turned into Twelve".

44. "Pole Balancing" performed by women.

46. "Duet Gymnastic Feats" performed by Pan Lianhua and another acrobat.

47. "Bending a Stiff Bow" performed by Zhang Shaojie.

49. "Throwing Torches to Each Other on Horseback" practised by young circus performers.

48. "Trio Pagoda of Bowls" performed by Dai Wenxia and others.

50. "Pagoda of Bowls".

mainly of a rope. In modern times the rope has been superseded by wire which is more durable and smaller in diameter, hence the act is also called "Wire Walking". "Wire Walking" was considered rather monotonous for a long period, but recently many new developments have been made. Skills, far more difficult than before have been devised, and a rich variety of new items have been developed. Now "Wire Walking" items in China consist of two major categories: "hard wire" and "soft wire". The two ends of the "hard wire" are usually equipped with springs; hence called "spring wire". Performers demonstrate diverse movements, usually dancing on the hard wire, utilizing the elasticity of the spring. "Soft wire" refers to the fact that the wire swings loosely between two supporting racks. A performer standing on this soft wire will waver slightly and, with the aid of such wavering, balance himself. In this position he performs kicking bowls and miscellaneous other feats and comic acts. Many outstanding performers have appeared on both "hard wire" and "soft wire", presenting the fascinating acts, "Sword Dance on Wire" and "Somersaults on Wire". The former closely combines the traditional art of sword play with balancing skills on a wire, prominently featuring the special characteristics of assurance, accuracy and beauty in Chinese acrobatics. In the latter, performers do somersaults on the wire, executing the highly difficult skills of "front somersaults", "back somersaults", "continuous soft somersaults" and "straight-body somersaults in the air", holding the audience spellbound (Colour plates 28 & 29).

"Juggling Properties with the Feet" has a very long history in China. When doing this feat, a performer lies with his face up on a specially devised seat and kicks and catches various acrobatic stage properties. The art of "Juggling Properties with the Feet" has been much improved since Liberation. New stage props, new techniques and new forms have steadily appeared and many new acts have been created. People often call "Juggling Jars", "Juggling Vats" and "Juggling Tables" and the like, "Juggling Weighty Properties with the Feet". They call "Juggling Parasols", "Juggling Bamboo Tubes" and "Juggling Boards" and the like, "Juggling Light Properties with the Feet". "Juggling People" and "Juggling Ladders" have become an independent category.

In the 1950's "Juggling Light Properties with the Feet", performed by Quan Liandi of the Chongqing Acrobatic Troupe, caused a sensation in the realm of acrobatics. Shortly afterwards, various items of "Juggling Properties with the Feet" appeared in different parts of the country. The "Duet Juggling Vats" of Guangzhou, "Juggling Tables to Each Other" of Wuhan and "Juggling Fans" and "Juggling Tablecloths" of Hangzhou each has its own characteristics. In particular, the "Duet Juggling Parasols" by the Li sisters of the Heilongjiang Acrobatic Troupe appeared in the 1970's. The whole performance centred around the display of skills with four parasols; sometimes the performers passed the parasols to each other; sometimes they juggled the parasols by themselves; the parasols on the performers' nimble feet seemed to be alive, doing somersaults, dancing or exchanging their positions. Finally, the technique of juggling two parasols with two feet brought the performance to a climax. Fluent choreography and virtuosity gave the audience aesthetic enjoyment (Colour plates 30 & 31).

"Balancing Gymnastics" by He Tianchong and Liu Xiaoling of the Chongqing Acrobatic Troupe ingeniously blends the art of juggling people with artistic poses. "Springboard Stunts and Juggling People" by Pan Sumei of the Shanghai Acrobatic Troupe is a new work of the 1980's. Utilizing the elasticity of the springboard, two little girls are brought in turn to the performer's feet.

They sometimes land horizontally, and sometimes perform somersaults. This blends the art of juggling properties with the techniques involving springboards and somersaults. Thus the item differs in imagery, difficulty and rhythm from the original items of "Juggling People" and "Springboard Stunts" (Colour plates 32, 33 & 34).

The daily increase of group acts is a major characteristic on the acrobatic stage of New China. This means that an additional number of performers display their skills simultaneously. Qualitative changes have also taken place in the images presented and in the execution of gymnastic skills. Consequently, a number of brand-new acrobatic acts have appeared. Take "Duet Pole Climbing" for instance. "Gymnastics on Fixed Pole" used to be done on a single pole and hence had its limitations. Since the "Duet Pole Climbing" of the Fighters' Acrobatic Troupe appeared in the 1950's, it has opened up new vistas for the art of pole climbing. Two long poles are erected on the stage at the same time and the performers, leaping to and fro between the two poles, execute many new gymnastic skills. For example, "Leaping from One Pole to the Other with a Full Turn", "Leaping Backward from One Pole to the other", "Two Performers Exchanging Positions on the Poles" and "Making Two Full Turns on the Pole". They look like silvery fish leaping out of the water and young swallows soaring into the sky. These difficult, graceful movements cannot be achieved on a single pole.

The appearance of "Poses on Chairs Stacked Atilt" has presented an image unrivalled by the former stage version of "Handstands on a Stack of Chairs". It displays varied and colourful pictures as well as many new techniques. This act differs from the former one in which a single performer does handstands on a vertical stack of chairs. The chairs in this new act are stacked atilt one on top of the other. Two of the four legs of each of the chairs are suspended, and each performer demonstrates his skills on a chair. With six people performing in harmonious coordination from bottom to top and doing handstands on a stack of seven chairs, it looks as if the centre of gravity inclines in one direction and breaks the law of balance; nevertheless, it does not tumble down. (Colour plate 35).

Animal masquerade performances have been handed down in China for many years. But only after the founding of New China were they presented on the acrobatic stage. For instance, the "Lion Dance", now very popular on the stage, was formerly a recreational show for holidays or festive celebrations among the common people in China. It was not regarded as a regular acrobatic act. After Liberation, the China Acrobatic Troupe was first to present the "Lion Dance" with a distincitve national folk tradition. They performed it with its charectersitic of difficult gymnastic skills. In the past three decades various acrobatic troupes have endeavoured to improve their skills in presenting the "Lion Dance". They solicited the guidance of folk artists, collected and studied folk data on this subject and, with constant improvement and refining, created the highly difficult techniques such as "Two Lions Tread on Balls Rolling Across a Seesaw", and "Lion Walks on a Rope", as well as "Lion Rolls a Ball", "Lion Performs on Stakes" and "A Boy Teases a Lion". They made the "Lion Dance" a representative example of Chinese acrobatics (Colour plate 36). In addition, there are the "Dragon Dance", "Teasing the Toad", "Flying Trident" and "Juggling with the Hands on Horseback". All these acrobatic acts have been devised on the basis of rediscovering traditional folk skills. They possess both rich national flavour and many new techniques, as well as a new style.

Borrowing from Chinese classical drama, dance and sports, new acts have been devised for acrobatic performances. For instance,

"Swinging Rings in Mid-Air", "Kicking the Shuttlecocks", "Wooden Horse Vaulting" and "Comic Tapping of Balls" have their origin in sports; "Silk Sling", and "General Guan Yu's Halberd Display on Horseback" are drawn from classical drama; "Colour Fans Contend in Beauty", "Sword Play on Horseback" and "Dance on Wire" are drawn from dance. Although drawn from sports or other performing arts, these acrobatic act differ from their original form when they are combined with the movements of acrobatic. For example, "Swinging Rings in Mid-Air" differs entirely from the "Swinging Rings" in gymnastics. A male performer doing a handstand in mid-air holds two rings in his hands while another male performer displays different acrobatic skills at the lower end of the rings. Although "Colour Fans Contend in Beauty" contains some movements of the fan dance, the aim is not to perform a dance. Instead, dance postures are used to conceal the secret of magic tricks. General Guan Yu was a renowned general in the Three Kingdoms Period (A.D. 220-265). There are many items about General Guan Yu in Chinese opera, presenting him as a hero with a dark red face, with eyes like a phoenix, fine bushy eyebrows like silkworms and a long beard. The circus act "General Guan Yu's Halberd Display on Horseback" does not portray the hero's personality through the developmet of the plot,

as in the opera. It features only traditional skills of horsemanship. The performer puts on a semblance of the general's countenance familiar to the people so as to make the presentation more grand and imposing.

Learning the advanced acrobatic techniques of other countries is also a factor in the development of Chinese acrobatics. But this does not mean indiscriminate imitation of foreign experience. Chinese acrobatics strives only to combine what is advanced in that experience with national style and traditional skills in order to create acrobatic acts which will be loved by the Chinese people. For instance, the act "On the Flying Trapeze" uses a popular modern power-driven rocket as a stage prop, and the rotating ladder frame facilitates the display of the beautiful human physique. But when it comes to performing skills, it uses the traditional "Poses on a Pole" as its basis. It also assimilates the new techniques of other countries with graceful Chinese national dances to form a marvellous tableau. The performers' makeup and costumes ingeniously use the images of flying devatas (goddesses) and celestial musicians and dancers from ancient murals in the Dunhuang Grottoes in Gansu Province, and the musical accompaniment consists of national classical melodies. As a result, an aerial presentation in Chinese style and grandeur has come into being.

Constantly Improving Skills

Acrobatics is a performing art with gymnastic skills as its core. It's performers have a tradition of endeavouring to perform difficult skills, and consistent practice has resulted in the presentation of Chinese acrobatics with a classical simplicity. Most of the traditional acrobatic presentations exhibit great skill

while making use of common, everyday utensils. Over the past three decades, in the spirit of constantly improving their skills, organizations and individuals determined to develop acrobatic arts have achieved distinguished results in developing most difficult, refined and unique skills and presenting performances which display assurance, accuracy and beauty.

In acrobatics the gymnastic skills using different parts of the human body can be boiled down to four essential skills: use of the waist, use of the legs, performing somersaults and doing handstands, with the last skill as the most important. All four essential skills have made rapid progress in recent years. Take handstands for instance, which used to be rendered only by male performers in the early years of New China. At that time, acrobats of "handstand propped up by a single arm" were regarded as rare experts. Now various troupes have a number of handstand performers with consummate skills. They are able to perform diverse kinds of handstands on moving bicycles, galloping horses or on a soaring pagoda of chairs. A handstand propped up with a single arm is no longer considered a highly difficult movement and many female performers do this pose with ease. They have practised and mastered handstands propped by a single arm while balancing pagodas of bowls placed in the shape of a cross, balancing bowls with the feet, throwing down wooden blocks one by one and three performers one on top of the other. Sometimes, a whole programme consisting of single-handed handstand skills is presented, including the hard-to-attain skill of going up and down a ladder. (Colour plate 37).

New developments have also been made in the other three essential skills, and quite a number of new acts have been composed, displaying the nimbleness, beauty and vitality of the human body. "Calisthenics" is one of them. Relying on her skill in using her waist and legs, a performer can bend her body into the shape of a ball or a ring. She can also do handstands on a flower-shaped stage prop and bend her body into three twists as if her bones were as soft as cotton. These acts are evolved from the traditional Chinese skills of soft-intrinsic exercises

(Colour plate 38).

"Jumping Through a Wooden Bucket", "Rolling with a Cup of Water" and "Pearl Maiden", although different in form from "Calisthenics", achieve the same effect. "Rolling with a Cup of Water" is usually performed by a girl in her early teens lying prostrate on a small oval table. Utilizing her skill in the use of her waist, she rolls over and over again, presenting diverse dance tableaux of grace and beauty. "Rolling with a Cup of Water" by Dai Wenxia of the Children's Group of the Guangzhou Acrobatic Troupe was performed in the following fashion: her left hand and both feet each supported a pile of gold-fish jars and her head balanced four decks of glasses filled with grape wine, while her right hand held her left foot to form a small "gateway". Her head and body went through the "gateway", making a 360 degree turn, while still balancing the gold-fish jars and the glasses. This performance exhibited her proficient skill, soft but tenacious waist and legs, and her excellent balance (Colour plate 39).

"The Pyramid" is the only acrobatic act which does not resort to stage props. Its movements include all the essential skills in the use of waist and legs and in doing somersaults and handstands. In general, it is divided into two categories: the greater pyramid and the lesser pyramid, depending on the number of performers on the stage. In the past three decades, techniques for performing this act have steadily developed. The "Lesser Pyramid" presented by the Cheng brothers and their sister has gradually worked out its own distinctive style, comprising 174 movements performed in six and half minutes. Neatly executed, it represents proficiency, precision, lively rhythm and presents a beautiful dance tableau.

The "Greater Pyramid" with many performers looks impressive, demonstrating precise and difficult skills. The "Pyramid of Nine

Acrobats" and "Quadrangular Seat Made of Clasped Hands" devised in recent years are breathtaking. The former presents nine performers supported by an acrobat of normal physique, showing extraordinary latent strength and courage. In the latter, a quadrangular seat shaped by the hands and forearms of two performers is created. Making use of the elasticity of the hands, they juggle the performer standing on the quadrangular seat into the air to do all sorts of somersaults. In this act the performer on the seat can make continuous, difficult somersaults with a 360-degree pirouette and two back somersaults with two twists, as well as combining somersaults with head-to-head, shoulder-to-shoulder movements of two performers, one standing on top of the other. These new routines have greatly enriched the content of "The Pyramid".

The art of "Jumping Through Hoops" has also made great progress. A performer jumps to and fro through a bamboo hoop erected on the stage, displaying a figure of health and beauty and the agility of the body. Formerly, an acrobat would jump through two hoops. Now new skills have been devised such as "Circling Through Three Hoops", "Jumping Backward Through Four Hoops", "Leaping over Two Hoops" and "Making Twists While Jumping Through the Hoop". Thus the performers' swallow-like litheness, vigour and nimbleness are featured (Colour plate 40).

The art of balancing is an important factor in many acrobatic items. Balancing skills have shown remarkable improvement, especially in such items as "Balancing on a Swaying Ladder", "Balancing on a Swaying Board", and "Treading on a Ball". "Balancing on a Swaying Ladder" uses an ordinary wooden ladder as the stage prop and the performers standing on the erect ladder do the routines of "Juggling with the Hands" and "A Tableau of Two Performers, One on Top of the Other". As the ladder is unsteady, without support

on any side, the performers on the ladder must readjust the centre of gravity at all times by the swaying of his waist and legs. "Balancing on a Swaying Board" is often performed in the following fashion: a round log is put under a wooden board about 0.6 metre long and 0.3 metre wide, and an acrobat standing on the swaying board displays various feats and supports several performers, one on top of the other. In "Balancing on a Swaying Ladder", two performers do headstands on head, and each with six hoops twirling on their hands and feet at the same time. The acrobat serving as the base rotates the ladder in a 720-degree pirouette. "Balancing on a Swaying Board" presents four performers one on top of the other, with the topmost performing somersaults and handstands. This has never been seen before. Many performers juggling with their hands can present their skills on a ball, and this increases the difficulty of skills. In Qian Zhongde's "Feats While Treading on a Ball", he juggles and catches small balls while treading on an unsteady big ball while continuing to maintain the balance of his body. His performance brims with wit and humour. Fan Xueqing demonstrates an extremely difficult example when he juggles and catches eight small balls on a small, narrow swaying board, thus setting a new record for "Juggling Balls" since ancient times. Zhang Jinlong of the Railway Corps Acrobatic Troupe balances "A Crystal Pagoda" created by glasses piled up on his forehead. This requires delicate balancing skill; with the slightest dislocation of a small wine glass, the whole "Crystal Pagoda" could tumble down. He has made the performance of this act more complex by shifting it onto a swaying board. So he must maintain his balance both above and below, with meticulous care. Recently he advanced one step further and added the movement of going up and down two ladders on the swaying board, and hence raised the multiple balancing skill to a new level (Colour plate 41).

The traditional art of juggling has been varied and colourful. Recently there have been improvements in skill and artistic innovations in form. "Plate Spinning" is an example of one improvement. Formerly, when a performer held three fine bamboo sticks with one hand to spin three plates, he was honoured as an expert. Now a performer can spin six plates with one hand. To give other examples, a performer used to kick one shuttlecock; now some performers can kick two shuttlecocks at the same time (Colour plates 42 & 43).

In the past, "Swinging Meteors" was considered to be a skill in the use of the hands; now a performer not only displays many new skills using the body and feet, but also performs somersaults while swinging meteors. New stage props such as meteor plates have also been designed and, when they are swung, it appears as if thousands of colourful lanterns were whirling in the night sky. Performers of kicking bowls boast a greater variety of innovations, some kicking on a swinging ladder, some on a wire and some on a unicycle; they vye with one another in demonstrating marvellous skills. Some juggling and kicking items have gradually developed into group performances and have provided new conditions for improving skills. For instance, kicking flying tridents, juggling jars and passing diabolos to one another are new techniques worked out for group performances.

Traditional acrobatics on poles such as "Balancing a Pole on the Forehead" and "Shouldering a Pole" have made new developments, apart from the above-mentioned "Duet Pole Climbing". Two performers doing handstands, juggling and catching properties, and performing somersaults and sometimes a dance tableau of four on a pole balanced on the forehead or on a shoulder — all these are new items worked out in recent years. The extremely difficult "Two Acrobats Exchanging Positions on the Poles", the art of which became lost for 1,000 years, has been revived and developed. Quite a number of acts have also been derived from the primary form of balancing a pole on the forehead or shoulder. This has greatly enhanced the artistic appeal of acrobatics on poles (Colour plate 44).

Vocal mimicry specialist Sun Tai, who won a gold medal award at the World Youth Festival in 1957, performed remarkably lifelike mimicry of the twittering of birds, chirping of cicadas, crying of infants and other diverse sounds. He almost succeeded in mixing the spurious with the genuine. Once, when Sun Tai performed in Romania, his vocal mimicry attracted a group of skylarks to chirp together with him. Formerly, only 30 to 40 kinds of sounds could be rendered in "Vocal Mimicry"; now, encouraged by the examples of Sun Tai and Zhou Zhicheng, performers can render more than 100 kinds of sounds. These include the sounds of windstorm and tide, cheers of a crowd of people, the sounds of military drilling of troops, of modern means of transportation and of shooting and explosion of weapons and ammunition. Consequently, the subject matter of "Vocal Mimicry" has widened and is therefore able to depict broader scenes of life, for instance, "Outpost at Coastal Defence", "Festivities" and "Morning in a Village". They can form an organic whole from diverse sounds, and listening to these, the spectators feel as if they were actually on the scene.

"Magic" is a major category in the field of acrobatics, often making up an independent performance. Many provinces and cities have formed professional magic troupes and groups in recent years, further promoting the innovations and inventions of magic tricks. After many years of refining and polishing the design of stage props, the presentation of tricks and the composition of items, "Traditional-Style Conjuring", "Folk Magic

Tricks" and "Miniature Magic Tricks" now appear entirely new. This has enhanced the aesthetic character of the items and filled them with a mystic flavour of oriental magic. Famous old magician Zhang Huichong has created, with artistic virtuosity, the feature-length acts "An Aquatic Box of a Hundred Jewels", "The Mermaid" and "The Vanishing Horse". These are all new acts with distinctive features. Since the 1960's, many magicians have fervently worked out medium-length magic acts on special subjects, for example, "Table-Tennis Balls Convey Friendship", which mainly presents magic tricks based on conjuring table-tennis balls. There are also "A Hundred Flowers Contend in Beauty" mainly conjuring flowers, and "Fishing" devoted to the conjuring of fish. These specialized acts break away from the old conventions of magic performances and make the performances more interesting. Each has its own style in stage design, combination of skills and forms of presentation.

"Magic" stresses the wonder of sleight-of-hand. This is shown by the younger generation of performers in New China. For instance, "A Ball Turned into Four" — the magic act emphasizing sleight-of-hand — has been developed into " One Ball Turned into Twelve". This act is performed without the cover of any stage prop; 12 light, hard, slippery balls appear and vanish between the performer's fingers. This cannot be achieved without several years of effort (Colour plate 45). In the "Changes of Thimbles" performed by Zhang Li, 30 multi-coloured thimbles appear on and vanish from the tips of her fingers, displaying proficient skill with refreshing novelty.

Ingeniously designed "Magic" items have often appeared on the stage. "Calligraphy and Painting Magic Show" by Fu Tenglong of Shanghai is one of the excellent works developed in the 1980's. He combines Chinese calligraphy, traditional painting and magic. The hen drawn on the blackboard is able to lay an egg and the egg becomes a chicken on the spot. The chicken instantly grows big and transforms into a big cock, which appears in the painting. "Mysterious Silhouette", also performed by him, is still more inconceivable. He asks a random spectator to ascend the stage, cuts out his silhouette from black paper and then opens a wooden box, already hung on the stage, and therein appears a silhouette exactly the same as the one he just cut out. The spectator is able to take his own silhouette when he leaves the stage, but remains puzzled by the magic act.

Circus and tamed animal acts almost became lost before Liberation. China has only a few professional circus troupes today, but many acrobatic troupes give circus and tamed animal shows. In the past few decades folk horsemanship has been revived and raised to a higher level. This includes such traditional skills as "Mounting a Galloping Horse in Eight Steps", "Mounting a Horse by Grabbing Its Mane", and "Handstands on Horseback". Also included are "Dipping Below the Horse's Belly with the Feet Still in the Stirrups", and "Sabre Display on Horseback". "Group Horsemanship", "Somersaults on Horseback" and "Martial Tableaux on Saddled Horses", performed by the China Acrobatic Troupe, demonstrate skills of a fairly high level. Of greater originality is the act, "Juggling Properties with the Hands While on Horseback". It combines the traditional juggling skills such as brandishing a big flag, juggling balls and juggling a sword with horsemanship, to make the performance more lively. A still more thriling act is performed in the following fashion: two performers, both standing on horseback, juggle and catch six torches from each other. They have to estimate exactly the distance between two horses, how fast two persons can juggle and catch objects, as well as the balance between the performers and horses. Multiple contradictions are solved through the performers' consummate skills; this forms an artistic image of beauty to the delight of the audience.

In tamed animal shows, the traditional "Monkey Show" has made rapid progress. A number of tamed monkey acts exhibiting diverse skills have been devised, including "Monkey Feats on a Wire", "Taming Monkeys and Sheep" and "Monkey Does Handstands on Chair". There are also performances of "Little Tamed Dogs", "Tamed Hounds","Tamed Ponies", "Tamed Camels" and "Tamed Bears". In these acts little dogs are able to jump through hoops, skip ropes, and perform a hurdle race. In others, hounds can "read characters" and "do arithmetic" and a little monkey walks on a wire with water buckets on its shoulders, rides with its playmates and does back somersaults on a bicycle. In still others a bear treads on a ball rolling across a seesaw, plays basketball and dances. Such performances astonish the spectators. The highlight is the act "A Tamed Giant Panda" by the young performer, Lu Xingqi, of the Shanghai Acrobatic Troupe. In a little more than a year, the clever, lovely giant panda has acquired the skill of riding on a wooden horse, kicking a wooden bucket, sliding down a slide, doing somersaults, and blowing a trumpet while on a bicycle. The precious panda's performance on the stage has written a new page in the history of tamed animals.

Eternal Youth and the Continued Emergence of Talented Acrobats

Art is created by people. The revival and development of Chinese acrobatics should be, first of all, attributed to a large number of folk artists from the old society. They represent the generation who, inheriting the past and ushering in the future, served as the mainstay in the ranks of acrobats in the early post-Liberation period. They pioneered modern acrobatics in socialist China. Their unique skills can rival their counterparts in other countries even though in the old society each of them had been in an abyss of miseries.

A famous cycling performer Jin Yeqin, who was a gold medal winner at the World Youth Festival in 1957 (Figure 79), went performing with his father at the age of 10, roaming from place to place in a desperate plight, semi-starved and dressed in rags. Sometimes he had to perform acts of cruelty and horror, and was filled with grief, indignation and a sense of humiliation.

Li Fengying, now Honorary Director of the Shandong Provincial Acrobatic Troupe, is a versatile acrobat. As an acrobat she was called "Peerless in Shandong Province", testifying to her unparalleled skills. Sold to a circus group at the age of eight, she had a miserable childhood under the whip of the boss of the group. After acquiring skills she became a ready source of money for the boss, but she did not have the slightest personal freedom.

Renowned artist of "Traditional-Style Conjuring", Yang Xiaoting, born into a poor family in Tianjin, began to learn magic from his master at the age of 12. After eight years of hardship, he became versed in the skill and had a good command of magic tricks. But it was difficult to earn a livelihood by selling one's art. He could not afford to buy the stage props of coloured porcelain objects and costumes, so he had to perform as an assistant for other magicians, year in and year out. He found it hard to support his wife and children. Finally he had to eke out his living by borrowing money and pawning things.

New China has brought a new, stable life to this large number of folk artists who went through all kinds of hardships and difficulties, providing them opportunities and conditions to give full play to their special skills. Profound changes have also taken place in their social status. They have become esteemed artists. Many were elected deputies to the national or local people's congresses or members of the Political Consultative Conference, and to participate in state affairs. In this new atmosphere they are in high spirits and plunge themselves into people's acrobatic work laying a solid foundation for the modern acrobatics of New China.

Take Yang Xiaoting for instance. Now he has plenty of opportunities to display his

79. Jin Yeqin's cycling performance

unique skills. In New China he has steadily rediscovered, improved and refined Chinese folk magic tricks. He has rapidly revived a number of traditional magic acts and devised quite a number of new items. In the early 1950's the "Traditional-Style Conjuring" performed by him enchanted audiences at home and abroad. Foreign critics called it a "secret that cannot be unravelled". But Yang Xiaoting did not remain at a standstill. In 1959 he offered his masterpiece "Festivities with Surplus" as a tribute for the 10th anniversary celebration of the birth of New China. Its title conveyed a deep significance. In Chinese language "surplus" and "fish" are two characters of the same sound but with different meanings. "With surplus" means "abundance", "prosperity", and "inexhaustible resources". Making a pun of "surplus" and "fish", Yang Xiaoting conjured up golden fish all over the stage to convey his warm love and congratulations for the motherland. "Festivities with Surplus", is a rare and exceptional act which was performed in the following manner: Yang Xiaoting, wearing a long robe of rich national colours and carrying an embroidered bed sheet sprinkled with golden patterns, stood with composure, on the stage. He spread out the bed sheet to show the audience nothing was concealed therein. Throwing it on his shoulders, he called out: "Hey presto!" All at once from under the sheet he took out four glass bowls filled with luxuriant plants and fish swimming in water. When there were too many things for the eye to take in, he put the sheet on the stage and the sheet stood erect. Suddenly he removed the sheet, and there were six glass fish jars of varying sizes, filled with water, stacked one on top of the other. The jars were also filled with swimming fish, and underneath the jars was a vermilion wooden pedestal. Bending down, he picked up a large brass brazier, its fiery flames shone all over the stage. In a twinkling, he again threw the sheet over his shoulders and took out a large tea tray with seven glasses on it, each filled with steaming, fragrant tea. At this moment the stage was dotted all over with objects he had conjured. Taking off his long robe, he patted all over his body to show that nothing was hidden therein, He took the sheet from his assistant's hands, threw it over his body and did a somersault on the floor. Standing up, he had a glass fish basin in his hands and inside the basin was water and in the water were fish and on the surface of the water were a pair of coloured toy mandarin ducks. The last movement was called "Taking Off Clothing to Present Gifts", a superb magic act. This set of Yang Xiaoting's magic tricks conjured up water and fire and more than 20 objects. When the objects were heaped up, they stood higher than the magician; they weighed more than his body, and the stage props consisted of slippery and easy-to-break glass vessels. It is impossible to perform this act without special techniques and hard-to-acquire essential skills (Figure 80).

Yang Xiaoting's stage experience has opened up vast vistas for magic shows. He is versed in performing both feature-length magic acts and miniature magic tricks when surrounded by viewers on all sides. He is in good command of the execution of magic shows with spectators nearby. He has handed down a valuable asset to the younger generation of magicians. At present three generations of magicians have matured under his guidance.

For many years Yang Xiaoting has performed with great zeal for audiences. He has left his footprints on Hainan Island in the south and at the northern frontiers. As a representative of the acrobats, he attended the National Conference of Outstanding Workers and the Third National Congress of Writers and Artists and was elected a deputy to the Third and the Fifth National People's Congresses. In his many performance tours abroad he has established friendship ties with friends and counterparts in other countries. He is an honorary member of the International Magic Society and has contributed to artistic exchange among peoples throughout the world.

Most acrobats of the older generation such as Yang Xiaoting, no longer perform

80. Traditional-style conjury "Festivities with Surplus" performed by Yang Xiaoting

on the stage. But they still ratain their youthful vitality in the performing arts, sum up their own experience, and untiringly train successors in the acrobatic arts. Their superb skills will take root in the younger generations of acrobats, thus preserving the eternal youth of the art.

Constant emergence of new talented acrobats is a salient feature in the field of acrobatics of New China. Since 1949, the state has invested a great deal of manpower and material resources to train acrobats. Thanks to the arduous efforts of the older generation, large numbers of young acrobats have rapidly become proficient. According to initial estimates of several key acrobatic troupes, each of them has, in general, trained three to six groups of students. These young acrobats account for more than two thirds of the total number of acrobats. In addition to learning acrobatics, they also attend courses in political study, general education, knowledge and techniques of other branches of art, and attain an all-round development morally, intellectually and physically. Thus they have matured into a new generation of acrobats. Many have even surpassed the older generation with their skills and have become a mainstay on the acrobatic stage.

The development of this new generation of acrobats consists of three periods.

The first group of such acrobats were orphans, or children of poor performers born in the old society. They followed their fathers, elder brothers or old-style acrobatic groups to roam from place to place from their early years. They had some training in essential skills. China's liberation ended their miserable childhood. Recruited into various acrobatic troupes, they studied and practised hard in their new surroundings and promptly showed their artistic talent. Xia Juhua, bowl-balancing artist of the Wuhan Acrobatic Troupe; Peng Xiaoyun, cyclist of the Railway Acrobatic Troupe; Pan Sumei, versatile performer of the Shanghai Acro-

batic Troupe; Zhou Renhai and Wang Guoli, jar tricks experts of the China Acrobatic Troupe are distinguished representatives of such acrobats.

Xia Huhua, originally named Xu, entered the Xia family's circus group at the age of five. Nominally she was the foster-daughter of the group boss, but actually the boss used her as an implement to make profit. She was less than 12 in 1949 at the time of Liberation. After joining the Wuhan Acrobatic Troupe, she gradually freed herself from the restrictions of the feudal relationship of foster father and daughter, and became an independent artist. She practised with painstaking effort and surmounted every difficulty in the artistic execution of the act "Pagoda of Bowls", rendering a refreshing and original performance. Her presentation was awarded a gold medal at the World Youth Festival in 1957 and won glory for the country. Not halting at this success, she combined the "Pagoda of Bowls" with calisthenics and devised many extremely difficult, graceful movements. Since ancient times performers have balanced bowls with their head, but none ever thought of removing the bowls from their head with their feet while doing a handstand. It was Xia Huhua who first devised and grasped the new skills of "Removing Bowls with the Feet When Balancing a Pagoda of Bowls and Performing a Handstand". Today, this act covers a rich variety of content and form. It is Xia Juhua who initiated this improvement. She was elected outstanding worker and national people's deputy several times. She was a deputy to the Fifth National People's Congress and member of the Standing Committee of the National People's Congress. She was elected Chairman of the Association of Chinese Acrobats at the age of 44. She is probably the youngest chairman of various national asscociations in the field of literature and art (Figure 81).

The second group of new acrobats were

81. "Pagoda of Bowls" performed by Xia Huhua

trained between the 1950's and 1966, prior to the "cultrual revolution." During this period of time major acrobatic troupes in various provinces, municipalities and autonomous regions, with the support and financial aid of the government, ran acrobatic courses to train performers in a planned way. They provided a good environment for practising skills and invited experienced acrobats as coaches. Many workers, peasants, intellectuals and artists sent their children to attend these acrobatic courses which ran from five to seven years. Special staff members were assigned to care for the daily life of the students. The state provided clothing, board, lodging, travelling expenses and facilities for practising skills. Most teachers of acrobatic skills had a bitter experience when acquiring skills in the old society. Recalling the past, they felt a sense of duty in training successors in the acrobatic arts for the motherland, and so threw all their energy into the work. They took minute care of the students' daily life and did their best to make the students proficient at the earliest possible time. Some teachers lived with the students and, when practising skills, some coaches were injured several times for the sake of protecting the students. The teachers were tireless in teaching and the students studied diligently. The relationship between the teachers and students was one of harmony, superseding feudal relations between masters and apprentices in the old days. The well-known proverbs "I would rather give him a loan of 10 yuan than pass on my art" and "when the apprentice acquires skills, the master will be starved to death" which were prevalent in the acrobatic profession in the old society have vanished.

Guided by the new principle of training, the students had excellent conditions for study and acquired substantial essential skills and a wide range of knowledge. Quite a number of students have distinguished themselves in one particular branch of skills. Many others have become experts in one thing and good performers at many. For instance, Xue Jingjing of the Shanghai Acrobatic Troupe specializes in "Handstands"; her "Mounting and Descending Stairs While Performing a Single-Handed Handstand", "Throwing Off Bricks One by One While Performing a Single-Handed Handstand", and "Waving Hoops with Hands and Feet Simultaneously While Performing a Single-Handed Handstand on a Revolving Table" display unique skill and have strong artistic appeal. Pan Lianhua of the same troupe is a verstile young acrobat. He specializes in "Cycling", "The Pyramid", "Kicking Bowls", "The Flying Trapeze" and in comic performances. The "Duet Gymnastic Feets", performed by him and another acrobat, is full of humour and demonstrated a series of extremely difficult head-to-head skills. (Colour plate 46).

Children of families with several generations of acrobats account for a large proportion of the new talent in the field of acrobatics. The tradition of children taking over their father's profession plays a positive role. "Heavy Halberd Zhang" who performed on the pleasure grounds in Tianqiao (the Bridge of Heaven), in the southern section of Beijing, is one example. His son, Zhang Yingjie, is noted for bending a bow and lifting a heavy halberd, and his grandson Zhang Shaojie's muscular strength also surpasses that of other players. Zhang Yingjie was the first performer who presented the act "Bending a Bow and Lifting a Heavy Halberd" on the acrobatic stage in New China. Bending a stiff bow with a drawing force of 80

kilogrammes, he applies some vigorous but graceful movements of traditional martial arts in the display of skills with a single bow. The pose "Bow Spreads Out Like a Full Moon" represents a tall, straight stance of vigour and vitality. He has also devised the new routine of "Bending Five Bows at the Same Time". He simultaneously bends five stiff bows with his head, hands and feet, and the total drawing force amounted to 400 kilogrammes. The act, "Bending Bows and Lifting a Heavy Halberd" performed by his son Zhang Shaojie of the China Acrobatic Troupe, has made some breakthroughs and innovations in both skill and muscular strength (Colour plate 47).

Young performers, who have come forward since 1966, and especially since 1976 after the smashing of the Gang of Four, represent the youngest generation of acrobats. They possess health and beauty, and are full of vitality. Quite a number of them have surpassed their predecessors. The newest, most difficult and beautiful skills are often executed by this generation. Both the children's acrobatic groups of Liaoning and Guangzhou and the circus group of the China Acrobatic Troupe have been trained during this period. The above-mentioned Dai Wenxia, of the Children's Group of the Guangzhou Acrobatic Troupe, is a performer who graduated a short time ago. "Rolling with a Cup of Water" which she rehearsed under the guidance of Cui Liangyu, her teacher, raises this traditional item of calisthenics to a new level.

At the Fifth Louis Merlin International Acrobatic Contests, held in France in November 1981, Dai Wenxia's "Rolling with a Cup of Water" won "The First Prize of the Mayor of Chartres" for the individual performance (Figure 82). "Trio Pagodas of Bowls" by Dai Wenxia and her two associates won the first prize for a team performance, "The First Prize of the President of the Republic" (Colour plate 48). The three young per-

82. Cui Liangyu, a coach, guides Dai WenXia
in practising "Rolling with a Cup of Water"

formers are all excellent students of Cui Liangyu.

Chinese acrobats won three gold medals at the Sixth World Acrobatic Festival of Tomorrow held in Paris in January 1983. The three presentations were: "Plate Spinning" performed by Wu Min and others of the Hangzhou Acrobatic Troupe, "Juggling Properties with the Feet" by Wang Hong of the Heilongjiang Acrobatic Troupe and "Kicking and Balancing Bowls on a Unicycle" by Gao Jin of the Shenyang Acrobatic Troupe. The Appraisal Committee acclaimed the Chinese performance to be high in artistry and poetry, and to give the audience aesthetic enjoyment.

"Duet Pagodas of Bowls" and "Fourteen Acrobats on a Stack of Chairs" of the Guangzhou Children's Group and "Ladder on a Flying Trapeze" of the Liaoning Acrobatic Troupe, as well as "Group Horsemanship", "Juggling with the Hands on Horseback" and "Feats on the Trampoline" of the

China Acrobatic Troupe, are all excellent acts by children and young performers. Other acrobatic troupes have also trained a considerable number of expert performers. The Three Qian Brothers of the Nanjing Acrobatic Troupe excel in "Juggling with the Hands". One of them is able to throw up and catch seven badminton rackets and another can throw up and catch nine sparkling plastic hoops. They surpass the performance of "Seven Swords Pile Up and Leap High" as described in ancient records (Colour plates 49 & 50).

There is a folk saying: "As in the Yangtze River the waves behind drive on those before, so each new generation surpasses the last one". Continuous training of new and talented artists is the fundamental guarantee for the flourishing of acrobatics. Up to the present, this task has been mainly done by the training courses run by acrobatic troupes in different places. This style of training has achieved great results and acquired plenty of experience, but without unified, overall regulations. The First Congress of Chinese Acrobats held in 1981 made a suggestion to prepare the conditions for establishing a national school of acrobatics and circus.

It can be conceived that the acrobats in New China will make striking progress, with one generation surpassing the other. This age-old acrobatic arts will surely shine like a bright pearl in new splendour.

中国杂技古今谈

傅起凤

*

外文出版社出版
（中国北京百万庄路24号）
外文印刷厂印刷
中国国际图书贸易总公司
（中国国际书店）发行
北京399信箱
1985年（16开）第一版
编号：（英）7050—63
00765
7—E—1840P